Principles of
Catholic Theology

BOOK 1

Principles of Catholic Theology

Book 1, *On the Nature of Theology*

THOMAS JOSEPH WHITE, OP

The Catholic University of America Press
Washington, D.C.

The paper used in this publication meets the
requirements of American National Standards for Information
Science—Permanence of Paper for Printed Library materials,
ANSI Z39.48–1992.

∞

Cataloging-in-Publication Data is available from the
Library of Congress

ISBN: 978-0-8132-3693-3

Contents

Preface

The small book you are now holding is the first in a four-book set bearing the name *Principles of Catholic Theology*. The primary goal of this set is to explore central mysteries of the Christian faith from both the perspectives of natural reason (book 2) and divine faith (books 3 and 4). However, it seemed appropriate to begin this larger collection of theological investigations by lingering a little while on questions concerning the nature of sacred doctrine itself, as Aquinas does in his first question of the *Summa*.

Hence, I present in this book—although not in a systematic or complete manner—a set of reflections on sacred theology: what it is and how it should be pursued. The approach is deeply informed by the general principles of Aquinas but also seeks to be responsive to and in part informed by various concerns of the 21st century academy. Inspired by Aquinas, this book seeks explore questions that can arise for the Catholic faithful, and indeed for honest seekers after truth more generally. It includes a description of a theological movement, Thomistic Ressourcement, which I hope will be clarifying both to my fellow travelers in Thomistic circles as well as theologians farther afield. This all being said, not everything within these pages either pertains to or requires adherence to the mind of St. Thomas; the fundamental principles of Catholic theology apply to all of us who accept divine revelation and seek to penetrate its inner rationality, whatever our theological school.

The further books of the *Principles of Catholic Theology* have already been planned and, as of this writing, are in the process of being executed—to have a further understanding of their scope and intention, please read on to the Introduction at the start of this book and the entire set. My hope is that readers of these essays will be encouraged to explore this understanding of theology carried out in the subsequent volumes. The second book of the set will be much longer than this one, and the third and fourth longer still. I am aware that some scholars will have their sense of proportion offended by the publication of a multi-volume set of such unequal length; indeed, it offends my own sense of proportion. Nevertheless, the publisher prevailed upon me to make *On the Nature of Theology* its own (modest) volume so as to make it more easily placed in many hands.

There is a certain logic, moreover, that results from this division of material. Questions concerning the nature of theological inquiry—what we contemporaries usually call methodology—are important but can be addressed relatively briefly. Questions concerning the interaction of Christian claims and natural reason—the subject of the second volume—require rather more attention. Ultimately, a fulsome meditation on the sacred mysteries themselves—to "seek the things that are above" as St. Paul tells the Colossians—is the primary task of theology and deserves the greater part of our attention:

If then you have been raised with Christ, seek the things that are above, where Christ is, seated at the right hand of God. Set your minds on things that are above, not on things that are on earth. For you have died, and your life is hidden with Christ in God. When Christ who is our life appears, then you also will appear with him in glory. (Col. 3:1–4)

Theology is rendered fruitful today, as in the past, when it is allied with a living spiritual life in Christ and a pursuit of the contemplation of the mystery of God. It is not achieved first and foremost by seeking an adaptation of classical theological principles to ever-altering cultural norms and academic trends, but rather by contemplating the inner mystery of God, and the perennial truths of the Gospel revealed in Jesus Christ, through the medium of the apostles, their writings, and the tradition of the Catholic Church. Catholic theology is also enlivened by a consideration of the mysteries of grace present and operative in the Church as the living mystical body of Christ.

This collection seeks to contribute in its own modest way to such a tradition, and it does so by engaging with the classical thought of patristic sources, as well as Aquinas, always in conversation with a host of modern theologians of significant influence. My hope is that this book and those that follow may inspire others to consider—whether for the first time or in greater depth—the norms and conditions of Catholic theology as it may be most fruitfully practiced in our own era.

Acknowledgments

There are many people to thank for the preparation of the materials contained in this book and those that are to follow. Some of the essays were produced for the English-speaking theology journal *Nova et Vetera*. It is with gratitude that I would like to thank my co-editor of that journal, Matthew Levering, as well as the staff of the journal who have been engaged for many years in assiduous editorial work. John Martino at the Catholic University of America Press has been a great support in the production of this volume and others. I would also like to mention especially in this regard Sr. Karoline Marie To, RSM, who has helped me edit and prepare this volume and those that succeed it. I owe her a great debt of thanks.

This book is dedicated to the professors and staff of the Angelicum in Rome, who contribute to the ongoing research and teaching mission of the university.

Prior versions of these chapters appeared in the following publications, and are used with permission:

Chapter 1: The *Analogia Fidei* in Catholic Theology. Originally published as "The *Analogia Fidei* in Catholic Theology," *International Journal of Systematic Theology* 22, no. 4 (2020): 512–37.

Chapter 3: On Theology as *Sacra Doctrina*: Catholic Theology, The Pluralism of Catholic Schools, and the Ecumenical Aspect of Catholic Theology. Parts of this chapter were originally published as "On the Ecumenical Work of Reforming Christology: *Sacra*

Doctrina, Analogia Entis, and Kenosis," *Nova et Vetera* (English edition) 20, no. 2 (Spring 2022): 649–72.

Chapter 4: Thomism after Vatican II. Originally published in *Nova et Vetera* (English edition) 12, no. 4 (2014): 1045–1061.

Chapter 5: Ressourcement Thomism. Originally published in *The New Cambridge Companion to Christian Doctrine,* edited by Michael Allen (Cambridge: Cambridge University Press, 2022), 352–370. Reprinted with permission. © Cambridge University Press and Assessment 2023.

Principles of
Catholic Theology

Introduction

———:———

What does it mean to believe in Christianity? What are the core beliefs of Christians, those that mark them out as distinct and define them? Are these core beliefs credible, rationally defensible, for people today, or acceptable more generally for reasonable people of any age? One classical answer to the question of what constitutes core Christian beliefs points toward the Trinity as the central mystery of Christianity and, secondarily, toward the Incarnation.[1] In the New Testament, God's Trinitarian identity is revealed to humanity as Father, Son, and Holy Spirit, and a participation in the life of God is communicated to human beings through grace. The principal medium of this revelation and communication occurs by means of the Incarnation. God becomes human, the Word made flesh, in Jesus Christ.

However, these two mysteries of the Trinity and the Incarnation

1. See Thomas Aquinas, *Compendium of Theology*, ch. 2 [Translation by C. Vollert (St. Louis & London: B. Herder, 1947)]:

Faith is a certain foretaste of that knowledge which is to make us happy in the life to come. The Apostle says, in Hebrews 11:1, that faith is "the substance of things to be hoped for," as though implying that faith is already, in some preliminary way, inaugurating in us the things that are to be hoped for, that is, future beatitude. Our beatific knowledge has to do with two truths that our Lord has taught us, namely, the divinity of the Blessed Trinity and the humanity of Christ. That is why, addressing the Father, He says: "This is eternal life: that they may know You, the only true God, and Jesus Christ, whom You sent" (John 17:3). All the knowledge imparted by faith turns about these two points, the divinity of the Trinity and the humanity of Christ.

1

are linked to others: the election of Israel, the life of the Virgin Mary, the atonement and resurrection of Jesus Christ, his founding of the apostolic and Catholic Church, the institution of the sacraments, the life of sanctification, and the eschatological hope of salvation. From within these various mysteries of Christianity a clear order of intelligibility emerges, of initiatives taken on the part of God that benefit humanity and that reveal who God is. This intelligible order of mysteries, as expressive of divine wisdom and goodness, is the subject of the study of Christian theology.

Simultaneously, however, the mysteries of Christianity can and should be understood in harmony with our philosophical and natural understanding of the world, as well as in light of the consideration of alternative religious traditions and non-religious philosophical proposals. In short, one may rightly ask whether Christianity is credible or rationally defensible in the face of alternative conceptions of the truth, whether these alternatives stem from atheistic visions of reality or alternative religious claims. Why should one believe that reality as we commonly experience it is subject to a religious explanation? Is it reasonable to appeal to divine revelation to understand the world without ceding one's natural rational integrity? Is it reasonable to believe in God and to affirm that the human person has a subsistent, immaterial soul characterized by immaterial features of understanding and volition? When one uses modern historical-critical resources to examine the Christian revelation of the Trinity as it appears historically in Scripture and early Christian tradition, does that revelation appear to be something historically and conceptually coherent? Or does it appear to be a mere artifact of human reasoning, projected arbitrarily onto a historical background that cannot truly ground and withstand its imposition?

This second set of questions is concerned with the rational credibility of Christianity, and it is distinct from but also logically connected to the first set of questions, regarding the nature of Christian mysteries. The two are distinct, because the treatment of divine revelation (the mysteries of Christianity) entails the respect for the inner essence of that revelation, seeking to understand God on God's own terms, so to speak, while the treatment of the potential credibility of Christianity begins from human subject matters of reflection (common human experience and natural philosophical reflection on it) and seeks to demonstrate the potential compatibility of natural knowledge of the world with the claims of Christian revelation. The former science pertains to *sacra doctrina*, the consideration of divine things that can only be known in virtue of divine revelation and the grace of faith that proportions human understanding to that revelation. The latter science pertains to apologetics, human reason that considers the potential alignment of natural philosophical-historical reflection and divine revelation, even as these two sources of understanding remain distinct from one another. The latter science (apologetics) presupposes supernatural faith in Christian revelation, because one cannot seek to understand philosophically and historically what one does not first understand theologically. However, the latter science is conducted through the medium of what may broadly be termed "Christian philosophy." By the latter term I mean natural reasoning that is subject to Christian influences, not because it receives its first principles, modes of argument, or final conclusions from Christian revelation, but only in the sense that the natural mode of reasoning in this case adverts to and considers actively the rational plausibility of divine revelation, to which the reasoning person in question, *qua philosopher or historian*, is sympathetic due to the motives of supernatural faith. The point of apologetic reasoning is not primarily to convince or move the opinion of others. Rather, it is principally to consider with rigorous intellectual integrity, insofar as possible, the natural foundations for belief in Christian claims (such as the existence of the transcendent Creator, the existence of the spiritual soul, the logical coherence of Christian revelation) or the utter lack thereof.

This book, then, seeks to consider the nature of theology as a science of divine revelation. It is the companion volume to a second in this series, one that will consider the reasonableness of Christianity, that is, the relation of Christian theology to human philosophical rationality more generally considered. This inquiry, in two parts that are two distinct books, is conducted, then, through a set of interrelated essays that are thematically connected with one another.

This first book, *The Principles of Catholic Theology* Book 1, considers the nature of Catholic theology, the connection of mysteries in their intelligible order, the nature of various schools of theology within the Catholic tradition, the ecumenical exercise of dogmatic theology (wherein Catholics can take account of ideas about revelation presented by Orthodox or Protestant theologians), and the heritage of the Thomistic tradition in Catholic theology.

The second book, *The Principles of Catholic Theology* Book 2, is composed of four interrelated parts pertaining to the rational credibility of Christianity. The first part considers the problem of religious explanations of reality. Should one be open to the very idea of a religious understanding of the world we experience around us, and if so, what should we make of the claims of contemporary naturalist atheism? Can one reasonably prefer one religious vision of reality over another, and should one take revelation seriously as a potential source for knowledge about reality? Does doing so lead necessarily to the compromise of one's intellectual integrity as a reasonable person? The second part examines the related question of rational, demonstrative arguments for the existence of God and for the immaterial subsistence of the spiritual soul of the human person. The third part examines the historical scriptural and patristic unfolding of the Church's basic Trinitarian claims. It argues that the very idea of the Trinity is contained historically in New Testament revelation, rightly understood by the early Catholic Church, and is logically coherent, as well as intrinsically interesting to natural philosophical reason, insofar as it claims to tell us something about the inner identity of God in himself that we could not otherwise know by natural reason but that is profoundly naturally desirable for us to know. The fourth part considers the witness of Catholic saints as a reason for philosophical motivation to treat Christian revelation with intellectual seriousness, so as to engage with it as a possibly true revelation. This last part also examines the philosophical grounds for our natural desire to see God, a desire that is met in a certain way by the Christian revelation of the supernatural possibility of the vision of God in his essence, the beatific vision. A final coda in this second volume considers the challenge of Nietzsche's criticism of Christianity and the question of a grounds for truth, whether stated in philosophical or theological terms, in a supposedly postmodern epoch.

Taken together these two books seek to provide an extended thematic sketch or broad intellectual suggestion of the integral relation of supernatural faith and natural reason, so as to consider how one might reasonably pursue the study of divine revelation and simultaneously perceive its profound harmony with philosophical understandings of the human condition and of created reality more generally.

At the same time, this first book can stand on its own as a reflection "On the Nature of Theology," and so it is published as a single introductory volume that may prove useful for those concerned distinctly with the subject matter of Catholic theology. It is the first not only in a set of two but is followed by successive volumes. The second volume, as noted, pertains to the "Rational Credibility of Christianity." The third in the series is concerned with principles of Catholic theology regarding "God, the Trinity, Creation, and Christ," while the fourth volume is concerned with "the Church, Mariology, and Nature and Grace." Since these volumes are connected to one another thematically in a single collection, we should seek to explain briefly what is meant by "Principles," how one might understand the revelation of theological "first principles" and the order among them, and why this overarching set of essays is arranged in the order it is, given our contemporary theological context, namely in light of themes that emerge in modern Catholic theology in the wake of the Second Vatican Council. I wish to revisit these modern themes in light of principles found in classical scholastic theology, and especially in the thought of Thomas Aquinas and in the Thomistic tradition. These broader thematic considerations are applicable equally to the first two volumes on the nature of theology and rational credibility, and to the subsequent volumes concerned with other more ultimate topics of theology, such as the Trinity, Christ, and the Church.

ON FIRST PRINCIPLES

Aristotle generally employs the notion of a "principle" in a two-fold sense, one that is epistemological and another that is metaphysical.[2] In the epistemological sense, the notion of a first principle pertains not per se to a logical premise (the first proposition in a chain of valid reasoning), but to an idea or notion of something primary in reality and that helps one organize one's thought in a scientific or explanatory way.[3] For instance, the notion of the hylomorphic

2. See Aristotle, *Metaphysics*, V, 1, 1012b32–1013a23, where Aristotle discusses six distinct senses of the word "principles," four of which have to do with the real causes or origins of things themselves and two of which have to do with scientific explanations, starting points of investigation, and demonstrations. He notes here that all ontologically real causes are first principles of a kind, though not all principles are causes. He goes on in the next paragraph (*Metaphysics* V, 2, 1013a24–36) to provide an account of causes, as distinct from principles, and notes that there are four such causes, providing initial descriptions of formal, material, efficient, and final causality. [All citations are from Aristotle, *The Complete Works of Aristotle*, ed. J. Barnes (Princeton: Princeton University Press, 1984).]

3. First principles thus have an impact on explanatory argumentation. Logically, one must argue from first premises to final conclusions, and both of these (premises and conclusions) can refer us to first principles (epistemological references for purposes of genuine explanation). The first principles of knowledge refer us in turn to ontological structures in reality. They articulate basic truths we come to know about reality. Understood in this way, first principles come both at the start of our knowledge of things and at the term. They are presupposed when we first make arguments, and our arguments can resolve by bringing us to greater understanding of principles. They can either serve as premises to good arguments, or they may be more ultimate truths about reality to which we conclude at the termination of reasoned arguments. The latter in turn help us explain the realities we experience in light of their proper causes, since the knowledge of principles refers us back to the things in themselves. Aristotle (in *Posterior Analytics* I, 3, 72b5–73a20) argues that there cannot be a regression to the infinite in the order of demonstration. Certain principles and definitions are known per se by pre-demonstrative insight (*nous/intellectus*) from the beginning and are necessary for demonstration. In *Metaphysics* IV, 3–8 (1005a18–1012b32) he studies the very first principles of knowledge (such

composition of all material bodies, as consisting of both form and matter, is a notion from which one can begin to provide a universal explanation of change and physical causation in material bodies. Every physical body has a natural form, as an individual species of a given kind, with characteristic properties and various material component parts, which imply at base a radical indetermination, a potency for mutability that Aristotle terms "matter."[4] The ontological distinction of the form and matter in material realities themselves are the *naturally real* compositional principles in themselves. Our way of understanding them, in a universal abstract science, so as to organize our thinking about the realities in a coherent fashion and so as to explain their specific form, characteristic properties, material potencies and alterations, provides us with first principles that are *epistemological.* The latter are meant to correspond to the former, in the sense that our thinking toward and in light of first principles "scientifically" is something that allows our thinking to correspond to the nature of the realities around us, understood rightly in themselves. Taken in this way we can reason *towards* first principles as we begin to understand the causes and essences of things in themselves, and we can reason *from* or *in light of* first principles as we understand what is secondary and derivative within realities in light of what is primary and most explanatory.

Thomas Aquinas, as well as other major scholastic figures, take up this notion of first principles in their understanding of theology as a scientific discipline as well as in their philosophical reflections.[5]

---

as the principles of non-contradiction and identity), which are then shown to be the foundations of all science and which imply an epistemological realism. In other words, the very basic initial and inevitable knowledge we all have of being qua being (of things existing), and their natures and properties (however vaguely apprehended) and the distinctions between them (understanding there to be irreducibly diverse beings with various natures and properties), tells us something true about reality itself, and it provides us with a true way of knowing reality initially so as, in turn, to study it progressively. See the study of Lawrence Dewan in his "St. Thomas and the Seed of Metaphysics," *Form and Being: Studies in Thomistic Metaphysics* (Washington, DC: The Catholic University of America Press, 2006), 35–46.

4. See the analysis of Aristotle, *Physics* II, 1–3, 192b9–195b30.

5. On the natural habits of understanding, science, and wisdom, which deal with

For example, in his philosophical metaphysics, Aquinas employs notions of form and matter, substance and property, actuality and potentiality, as well as existence and essence, to explain the compositional nature of various created realities. He likewise considers what
a human being is in light of various explanatory principles, such as
the notion of the spiritual, subsistent soul as the form of the body
(so that they are together one substance), the notion of faculties or
powers of the soul, the theory of the agent intellect as the source of
human abstract conceptualization and discursive reasoning, the notion of intellectual and moral habits as explanatory of the ethical life
of the person, and the notion of beatitude or happiness as the final
end of human existence.

Theologically, meanwhile, Aquinas makes use of the notion of
first principles by similitude, to indicate the inherent intelligibility and connectedness of the mysteries of God revealed in Christ.[6]
Here, critically, he notes that human beings cannot provide for
themselves or naturally attain to the subject matter of the study of
theology or *sacra doctrina*.[7] Rather, God must reveal himself to the
human community publicly in divine revelation (in Christ, Scripture, tradition, the teaching of the Church) and provide the internal illumination of supernatural faith, so that the human person can
consent to the truth of the propositions of faith, intellectually perceive their object (God in himself), and reason in light of the various
truths that God has revealed about himself and his creation.[8] Again,
we see the two-fold notion of first principles as pertaining both to
what is the case metaphysically (God in himself and the mysteries
of revelation) and to our epistemological frameworks of explanation
(the science of theology as a study of who God is and of what he has
accomplished in works of creation and grace).

principles known by natural reason, see *Summa theologiae* I–II, q. 57, a. 2. [All citations
of the *ST* refer to *Summa Theologica*, trans. English Dominican Province (New York:
Benziger, 1947).]

6. See *ST* I, q. 1, aa. 2, 7, and 8.

7. *ST* I, q. 1, a. 1.

8. *ST* I, q. 1, a. 3 and a. 7.

Generally speaking, in the volumes represented under the title *Principles of Catholic Theology*, I mean to signify this two-fold sense of first principles, as indicative both of metaphysical structures of reality (in the order of nature and in the life of grace) and of theological science, as a form of knowledge that seeks explanations of reality and that is conducted formally in light of divine revelation.

THE MEDIUM OF REVELATION AND DIVERSE SCHOOLS OF THEOLOGY

Of course by alluding to Aquinas's definitional understanding of first principles, in both theological and philosophical study, I have implicitly raised the question of normative methods in Catholic theology. Must all theologians be disciples of Thomas Aquinas or members of a Thomistic tradition of thinking in order to pursue a rightly ordered form of theological reflection? More discussion on this topic is provided below, but here we can already note why, at least in some very significant senses, this cannot be the case, if one understands *sacra doctrina* as Aquinas himself does and is attentive to the long-standing teaching tradition of the Catholic magisterium on this topic. And yet, as I will also mention briefly, the contributions of particular schools of Catholic theology, including the especially central contribution represented by Aquinas and the Thomistic tradition, are of capital importance for the vitality and exercise of Catholic theology.

The principles of Catholic theology (taken in the two-fold sense indicated above) are revealed primarily through Scripture, the prophetic and apostolic doctrine of ancient Israel and the early Church. This scriptural and apostolic teaching (apostolic *doctrina* in Latin) is preserved and interpreted within the sacred tradition of the Catholic Church, stemming from the time of the earliest post-apostolic literature and liturgical practices of ancient Catholicism. This tradition is developmental, and it must be understood across time in a logically coherent, progressive, and organic way, so that there is a broad consistency and intellectual, moral, and spiritual unity to the Church's internal life under the auspices and irradiation of the grace of Christ.[9] The tradition in question, then, stems from the life of the Church: all the baptized Christian faithful living in genuine communion with the successors of the apostles—the apostolic hierarchy—and it is represented especially by great figures of sanctity who arise down through time within the corporate life of the Church. Taken as such, sacred tradition in its dynamic vitality gives rise to a set of normative references embodied in a variety of organic expressions: the sacred liturgy, the ecumenical councils and decrees of the Catholic magisterium, the writings of doctors of the Church, the examples of the saints, and the devotional and ethical practices of the faithful. These indicate normative ways of interpreting and understanding the scriptural and apostolic deposit of faith. Evidently for there to be stability and continuity within this dynamic across time, it is necessary for the episcopal college, in communion with the bishop of Rome, who is the successor of Peter and Paul, to maintain a clear teaching legacy regarding all that pertains to the Catholic faith, which is typically referred to as the teaching magisterium of the Catholic faith.

Understood in this way, we can begin to elucidate a hierarchy of sources within the authoritative revelation of God conveyed to the Church.

(1) The original source of revelation is God himself, who is the first origin and final end of revelation, and who conveys his revelation

9. See on this matter the teaching of the Second Vatican Council in the Apostolic Constitution on Divine Revelation, *Dei Verbum*, ch. 8. Unless otherwise indicated, citations and translations of ecumenical councils of the Catholic Church are taken from *Decrees of the Ecumenical Councils*, ed. Norman P. Tanner (London and Washington, DC: Georgetown University Press, 1990), based upon the critical edition of G. Alberigo et al., eds., *Conciliorum œcumenicorum generaliumque decreta*, Editio critica, vol. 1, *The Œcumenical Councils: From Nicaea I to Nicaea II* (325–787), Corpus Christianorum Texts and Studies (CC-TS) (Turnhout: Brepols, 2006); vol. 2–1, *The General Councils of Latin Christendom: From Constantinople IV to Pavia-Siena* (869–1424), CC-TS (Turnhout: Brepols, 2013); vol. 2-2, *The General Councils of Latin Christendom: From Basel to Lateran V* (1431–1517), CC-TS (Turnhout: Brepols, 2013); vol. 3, *The Œcumenical Councils of the Roman Catholic Church: From Trent to Vatican II* (1545–1965), CC-TS (Turnhout: Brepols, 2010).

of himself through the medium of Scripture and apostolic tradition.

(2) This revelation is received, safeguarded, interpreted, and progressively better understood within the context of the Catholic Church's living tradition, which itself depends upon and is entirely relative to the essential form of revelation in Christ received from the apostolic teaching.

(3) The tradition of the Church, her authoritative interpretation of Scripture, is sporadically codified and expressed in dogmatic and doctrinal form down through the ages. The dogmatic teachings of the Church participate in and convey authentically the infallible teaching of God in divine revelation. They are genuine articulations of what is contained in the apostolic teaching, and are subject to it, not substitutes for it. Furthermore, dogmatic understandings of the Church, while essentially infallible, are non-comprehensive, meaning that the Church's understanding of the revelation and of the dogmatic expressions of faith can themselves develop dynamically down through time, although always in an organically consistent and propositionally coherent way.

(4) Schools of theology arise down through time that present Catholic Christianity with concentrated proposals for better understanding the content of divine revelation faithfully, in light of Scripture, tradition, and the authoritative teachings of the Catholic magisterium. Because these various schools begin from a common basis of consent to the principles of divine revelation (in the two-fold sense mentioned above) they each share a broad similitude of reasoning and a common set of theories or theses, in regard to the practice of Christian theology. No such school can claim to be the definitive or final arbiter of Catholic truth precisely because each such school takes its starting points or first principles from the above-mentioned antecedent sources of apostolic teaching, and authoritative interpretation.

Nevertheless such schools of thought may also differ considerably based on a variety of factors: how they interpret the formal content of the revealed mysteries as maintained and promulgated according to the common faith of the Catholic Church, how they make use of historical sources (including the interpretation of Scripture), theological precedents (such as when providing an interpretation of Augustine or Maximus the Confessor on a point of major theological significance), the use of philosophical instruments in the service of theology (for example, by making use of various scholastic or modern philosophical claims), and in virtue of what they take various precedent authoritative statements of the Catholic Church to include or imply, or not to include or imply. Some theologians may be more insightful also because of their inner spiritual life such that they are conformed more deeply to the mystery of God through love in such a way as to facilitate by their study and writing greater familiarity with God and contemplative understanding of God. Another basic criterion has to do with the consideration of the very essence of *sacra doctrina* and its organizational principles: what does one take theology to be about *principally* and how might one understand the diversity of principles in light of what is absolutely primary?

Once one understands the complex reception of the principles of Catholic theology in this light, it is easy to see why, even if no one theological school of thought could ever define the principles of Catholic theology (which are received antecedently), one might still privilege a given theological school of thought. If Aquinas is considered a "common doctor" of Catholic intellectual life and thus a kind of Greenwich time in Catholic theology, it is not only due to his sanctity but also due to the order in which he presents Catholic theological mysteries, his interpretation of Scripture and reception of precedent tradition, his unique capacity to cast intelligible light upon mysteries of faith through profound analysis, and his use of philosophical reasoning in the service of faith. Later theologians can take up reflection upon the principles of Catholic theology in ways identical to or inspired by Aquinas so as to arrive at a unified science of theology across time. Many theologians after Aquinas have done so in a myriad of ways, thereby constituting a longstanding school of thinking in the Thomistic tradition or indeed a variety of such schools. As we will note below, such thinking within a tradition normally does not permit its adherents to preserve a merely insular way of thinking hermetically sealed off from alternative viewpoints or from the new questions or philosophical and scientific proposals of a given age, but on the contrary, requires cyclical engagement of a dynamic kind precisely with such alternative challenges and with new questions.

THE ORDERING OF PRINCIPLES IN CATHOLIC THEOLOGY

In consistency with what we have presented above, we can note that when Aquinas treats the topic of the first principles of Catholic theology, he claims they are exhibited in the Nicene-Constantinopolitan Creed. The Creed represents a privileged expression of the normative teaching of the Catholic Church, itself formulated in light of the prophetic revelation given to Israel and the apostolic doctrine of the New Testament. In the Creed the revelation of the Trinity is asserted, Father, Son, and Holy Spirit, as well as the creation of all things visible and invisible by God. The Incarnation, passion, and resurrection of the Son of God are asserted, as well as the virginal conception and birth of Jesus by the Mother of God, the institution of the Catholic Church, her sacramental life (initiated at baptism), the final judgment, and the resurrection of the dead.

Theologians in the high medieval period typically disputed which mystery of Christianity was central to the study of Catholic theology, such that a central subject might serve as the organizing principle for the scientific analysis and contemplative understanding of all the others.[10] Understandably some claimed that the central mystery was the Incarnation, since it introduces us to the mystery of who God is, and what human nature is, in its most perfect mode. Others claimed that the Church, along with her sacraments, is the

10. See Ulrich G. Leinsle, *Introduction to Scholastic Theology*, trans. M. Miller (Washington, DC: The Catholic University of America Press, 2010), 120–81.

most central mystery, since it is only within the Church's ongoing life and teaching that we concretely encounter Jesus Christ, true God and true man, and thus come into communion with the Trinity. Aquinas, however, affirms that the fundamental truth that is central to Christian theology is that of the Trinity itself.[11] The Catholic faith is centered upon God in himself, as he is disclosed to us in Christ. The proper object of supernatural faith, then, is God in his essence, so that we are invited in faith to "see" into who and what God is, to know God personally, and to understand all of reality in light of God.[12] It is the Trinity who creates, who redeems, and who sanctifies. The consideration of all other Christian mysteries, including those of the Incarnation, the Church, and the sacraments, serves to further illuminate our understanding of God, as these mysteries reflect intensively the ongoing work of God, and thus the inner wisdom and goodness that are characteristic of the Trinitarian life of God in himself.[13]

When he considers the ordering of the principles of Catholic theology in this light, then, Aquinas typically employs a schema in which all things are seen to come forth from the Trinity and in which they are all called to "return" to the Trinity, in what Marie-Dominique Chenu termed an *exitus-reditus* pattern of thinking.[14] The *exitus* refers to all things that come forth from God or emanate from him in his creative power, wisdom, and goodness, and in the communication of his life of grace. The *reditus* refers to the vocation to beatitude and divinization to which all angels and human beings are invited collectively, in virtue of that same life of grace. The

---

11. *ST* I, q. 1, a. 7 affirms that God is the subject of *sacra doctrina*, while *ST* II-II, q. 1, a. 1 affirms that God in himself as first truth is the formal object known by the act of faith, which makes this subject intelligible. *ST* II–II, q. 1, aa. 6–10 affirm that the formal object of faith (God in his Trinitarian life, who is manifest in his various works of nature and grace) is best articulated in the principles of the Nicene Creed, as enunciated in the symbol.

12. *ST* I, q. 1, a. 3.

13. *ST* II–II, q. 1, a. 8.

14. See Marie-Dominique Chenu, *Toward Understanding Saint Thomas*, trans. A.-M. Landry and D. Hughes (Chicago: Henry Regnery, 1964), 304–14.

Summa theologiae can be read in this sense as a work that examines the theology of the divine economy. After first contemplating the mystery of God and the Trinity, Aquinas considers creation, and he focuses especially on angels and human beings, each created with a natural integrity but also created in a state of grace. His study of the fall of some angels and of the first human parents from grace leads to a consideration of the economy of redemption. In the second part of the *Summa* he considers in greater depth the nature of the human person and the moral life of human beings who are being redeemed by grace. In the third part he considers the Incarnation and the sacraments together as the principal remedy for human sin and as the supreme means of the mediation of grace, by which human beings may rejoin God. Although Aquinas died before he could complete his eschatology, it is clear that the orientation of the *Summa* was ordered to the consideration of the "last things": personal and final judgment, heaven and hell, the universal resurrection. This ordering of all things back to God is envisaged under the aegis of a Trinitarian understanding of humanity, wherein God is meant to become by grace the final destiny of human persons who are gathered into the collective, eschatological life of the Church.

One can contest this interpretation of the order of the principles of Catholic theology, and indeed some have argued that Aquinas is concerned in the *Summa theologiae* principally with the study of God, of man, and of the God man (Christ), so that the study unfolds in an order that is merely metaphysical, not economic.[15] However, the evidence from the accompanying *Theological Compendium* seems to confirm the original interpretative hypothesis, as Aquinas also there considers the Trinity, the creation, the final end of the creation, which is the rational creature and its beatitude, and then considers the eschatological destiny of human beings, in the life of the resurrection. The mystery of Christ and the redemption, as well as his final judgment of all human beings, is understood within the con-

15. See the criticisms of the Chenu schema by Rudi te Velde, *Aquinas on God: The 'Divine Science' of the* Summa Theologiae (Aldershot: Ashgate, 2006), 10–18, 31.

text of this ontologically prior mystery of the *exitus* and *reditus* of all things from and unto God.[16] Christ is at the center of the re-creation of all things, so that the theology of Aquinas is Christocentric in a real sense, but this is qualified by the more fundamental theocentricism of his vision, in which the Trinity is the core mystery of the Christian faith. In Catholic theology, one does consider metaphysically both God and man, as well as the God-man, but this occurs within a larger framework of metaphysical emanation, in which God communicates being and grace to the world in order to beatify the

16. Significantly, Aquinas completes his exposition of the Catholic faith in chapter 246 of the *Compendium of Theology* by claiming in conclusion that the aforementioned teachings are comprised in the articles of faith, themselves represented in the symbols of the Apostles' and Nicene Creeds. Interestingly Aquinas acknowledges contemporary debate regarding the number of principles enunciated overtly in the Creed, and argues that rather than fourteen, there are twelve. This interpretation has to do with the fact that he interprets the mystery of the Trinity as pertaining to one principle rather than three:

> Faith has to do with truths that surpass the comprehension of reason. Hence, whenever a new truth incomprehensible to reason is proposed, a new article is required. One article pertains to the divine unity. For, even though we prove by reason that God is one, the fact that He governs all things directly or that He wishes to be worshiped in some particular way, is a matter relating to faith. Three articles are reserved for the three divine persons. Three other articles are formulated about the effects produced by God: creation, which pertains to nature; justification, which pertains to grace; and reward, which pertains to glory. Thus seven articles altogether are devoted to the divinity.
> Concerning the humanity of Christ, seven more are proposed. The first is on the incarnation and conception of Christ. The second deals with the nativity, which involves a special difficulty because of our Lord's coming forth from the closed womb of the Virgin. The third article is on the death, passion, and burial; the fourth on the descent into hell; the fifth on the resurrection; the sixth on the ascension; and the seventh treats of Christ's coming for the judgment. And so there are fourteen articles in all.
> Other authorities, reasonably enough, include faith in the three persons under one article, on the ground that we cannot believe in the Father without believing in the Son and also in the Holy Spirit, the bond of love uniting the first two persons. However, they distinguish the article on the resurrection from the article on eternal reward. Accordingly, there are two articles about God, one on the unity, the other on the Trinity. Four articles deal with God's effects: one with creation, the second with justification, the third with the general resurrection, and the fourth with reward. Similarly, as regards belief in the humanity of Christ, these authors comprise the conception and the nativity under one article, and they also include the passion and death under one article. According to this way of reckoning, therefore, we have twelve articles in all.

human person, and in which the Incarnation, atonement, and resurrection take place in order to propel human beings into the heights of Trinitarian life.

This theological vision of the nature of theology and its principles deeply informs the essays in the volumes of this collection. At the same time, the order is slightly different for reasons we will explain below, which have to do principally with the post conciliar context of Catholic theology in the wake of the Second Vatican Council document *Lumen gentium*, which proposes a theocentric vision of the Church and understands the Church herself in light of God's deeper vision for the human race, one in which all of humanity is invited to beatitude in Christ.[17] I will turn to this topic shortly but first must consider briefly an essential and related attribute of the science of theology: the role of dialectic in regard to the elaboration of principles.

SCIENCE AS CONSISTING IN THE CONSIDERATION OF BOTH PRINCIPLES AND DIALECTIC

As is well-known, medieval scholastic theology was frequently structured around the consideration of disputed questions. Aquinas, like others, often frames his core treatment of controversial questions in theology by prior consideration of opposed positions and ultimate responses to those positions offered in light of his core considerations. This intellectual approach is clearly influenced historically by the example of Aristotle, who in his major philosophical treatises typically introduces in the first book of the work a variety of opinions or diverse positions on the topic developed by anteced-

---

17. See Vatican Council II, Dogmatic Constitution, *Lumen gentium* (1964), ch. 1 which establishes an understanding of the Church cast in the primal light of the Trinity and Christ. The visible Church is taken into consideration in an economic and historical fashion in ch. 2. Here in sections 14, 15, and 16 we encounter a series of concentric circles. The baptized Catholic faithful form the inner nucleus of the life of the Church in time and creation (section 14), but God's designs of ecclesial salvation in Christ reach out (section 15) to other baptized Christians, to other religionists, and to all people of good will (section 16). Indeed the missionary mandate of the Church is universal (section 17).

ent philosophers, prior to the elaboration of his own views. Aristotle furthermore typically considers objections to his positions along the way and seeks to refute those positions in light of the principles of philosophy that he claims to have uncovered or brought to light by means of his investigations.

This process is what we mean to denote broadly in speaking of intellectual "dialectic": the consideration of objections, alternative positions, and diverse intellectual opinions already present in the broader culture of humanity. Such dialectic is not a free-standing or independent intellectual activity, whether in philosophical or theological reasoning. It does not discover or instantiate anything in itself, and it does not provide *intrinsic* evidence or reasonable warrant for belief in principles of any kind. However, it does serve to illustrate, verify, and defend the intelligibility and rational warrant of various principles by demonstrating their viability in the face of alternative proposals and by showing objections against those proposals to be without grounds or warrant.

For instance, the dialectical consideration of Plato's theory of forms is not a sufficient condition for the elaboration of an Aristotelian conception of universal abstraction by the agent intellect. In refuting or raising problems with regard to the former, one can derive intrinsic understanding of the latter. However, it is only because one has a prior understanding of the latter (an Aristotelian-Thomistic argument for and analysis of the agent intellect as the source of universal abstract notions) that one can rightly criticize the Platonic theory of forms and defend the Thomistic positions on epistemology from various kinds of Platonic-Augustinian criticism. In doing so one strengthens the understanding of the principle in question and explores the greater reasonableness of its affirmation by way of a comprehensive philosophical reasoning.[18] Likewise, one might consider the argument of Apollinarius, that the affirmation of a human soul in Christ would stand in fundamental ontological oppo-

18. See, in this regard, Aquinas, *Summa contra Gentiles* II, trans. J. Anderson (Garden City, NY: Doubleday, 1956), chs. 73–78.

sition to the acknowledgement of his divinity as the uncreated Logos of God.[19] One cannot derive from Apollinarius the notion of the hypostatic union as comprised of one person subsisting in two natures, such that the genuine human intellect and will of the man Jesus are those of the divine person of the Son, subject to his divine wisdom and will, in virtue of which he is one with the Father and the Holy Spirit. However, once one has explored the contours of this theological mystery (the principles that one may use to indicate however obliquely the mystery of the Incarnation), then one can refute the Apollinarian vision by showing rightly that the presence in Christ of the fullness of the Godhead does not stand at odds in any way with the plenitude of his human nature and its perfection. On the contrary, precisely because he is God, Christ's human soul is inundated with the greatest intensity of grace, and in virtue of this mystery, he is the most perfect of all human beings. The perfection of Christ's divinity as true God and the perfection of his humanity as true man are not only not mutually opposed ontological truths, but are in fact mutually related in a profound way. The human perfection is a sign and indication of the true deity of Christ. The living godhead of the Son present within him is the deepest source of his perfect humanity.[20]

Such examples serve only to suggest that the ongoing work of theology, in its exploration of the principles of Catholic thought, is related to the ongoing disputations of a wider human culture, both within and outside of the Catholic Church. This wider culture includes not only the world of philosophy, science, history, and the arts, but also alternative religious traditions and of course alternative Christian confessional traditions, which often present ideas complementary to or convergent with those of Catholic theology, even as they also sometimes present themselves as providing a rival account of the truth of revelation over and against it. Dialectic does not provide the principles of the Creed, which we have noted above come

---

19. See Aquinas's consideration of this topic in *ST* III, q. 5, aa. 3–4.
20. See *ST* III, q. 7, aa. 1, 10, and 13.

from Scripture, tradition, and the magisterium. Nor does it provide the basis for a sound philosophical tradition that works serenely and scientifically in harmony with the Catholic faith. But deepening exploration and understanding of Catholic theological traditions and the philosophies that accompany these traditions also always occurs in relation to ongoing questions or challenges, as well new genuine insights, which emerge from the disciplines of the modern sciences, historical discovery, new philosophical investigations, alternative religious traditions, and ecumenical theological proposals from non-Catholic Christians. As such, dialectic rightly understood forms an essential part of the work of Catholic theology as a *condition* for the generation of deeper understanding, even if the essential principles of the Catholic intellectual tradition are not intuited or derived per se from the dialectical dimension of theological reflection.

THEOLOGICAL CONTEXT AND THE SECOND VATICAN COUNCIL

This multi-volume collection of essays has a systematic framework, passing from the topics of the Nature of Theology (Book 1) to the Rational Credibility of Christianity (Book 2) to those of God, Trinity, Creation, and Christ (Book 3), to those of the Church, Mariology, and Nature and Grace (Book 4). I will discuss this order of reflection in the final section of this introduction below, but first it is necessary to note briefly the theological context of the essays in these volumes.

A multi-volume work consisting of essays is not and should not pretend to be a singular volume of systematic theology. It consists rather in a loosely unified collection of ideas about dogmatic theology. As such, these volumes present systematic reflection across a spectrum of topics but not in a fashion that unites all the elements in each essay to every other.

It is obvious within the context of modern theology that this approach to theological ideas takes its inspiration from and is a kind of homage to major modern theological authors whose collections were published around the time of and in the wake of the Second Vatican Council. Karl Rahner's *Theological Investigations* is the most culturally significant of such collections, though one can also think in this context of Joseph Ratzinger's *Principles of Catholic Theology*, which my own title evidently alludes to. Bernard Lonergan's *Collections*, Hans Urs von Balthasar's *Explorations in Theology*, and Edward Schillebeeckx's *Revelation and Theology* volumes provide other examples.[21]

While these various works differ in many respects with regard to content and method, indicative in each case of the predilections of their authors, they nonetheless do each signal in some way a common set of concerns. Each attempts to explore a theological form of reflection that is emergent from precedent Catholic tradition, loyal to the core intuitions and aspirations of the Second Vatican Council, modern in tone and form of expression, and accessible to contemporary intellectual culture, while presenting traditional doctrinal ideas in ways that are intended to be sympathetic and compelling to modern people given their particular existential concerns and motivations. As such, these works can be seen as forming part of a larger intellectual context that surrounded the Second Vatican Council, in which they present interpretations of that event and its documents. The fact that these authors wrote in the form of essays is significant, since they were each seeking to discover new formats for the expression of Catholic theology in a contemporary idiom and were exploring Catholic theological positions on a host of new questions.

21. One can find a comprehensive reference to the English translation editions of the first of these works in Daniel Pekarske, *Abstracts of Karl Rahner's Theological Investigations 1-23* (Milwaukee: Marquette University Press, 2003); see, likewise, Joseph Ratzinger, *Principles of Catholic Theology: Building Stones for a Fundamental Theology*, trans. Mary Frances McCarthy (San Francisco: Ignatius Press, 1987); Bernard Lonergan, *Collected Works of Bernard Lonergan*, ed. F. Crowe, R. Doran, and others (Toronto: University of Toronto Press, 2000-present), vol. 4: *Collection*, vol. 13: *A Second Collections*, vol. 16: *A Third Collection*; Hans Urs von Balthasar, *Explorations in Theology*, vol. 1-5, trans. A. V. Littledale, A. Dru, and others (San Francisco: Ignatius Press, 1989-2014); Edward Schillebeeckx, *Revelation and Theology*, vols. 1 and 2 (New York: Sheed and Ward, 1967).

The Council had identified many of these topics: a Christological vision of the Church and an ecclesial vision of the collective vocation of the human race, the Catholic Church's own orientation
toward modern Christian ecumenism, the Church and the people
of Israel, her relation to non-Christian religions, the relation of the
Catholic Church to modern secularized political states, the nature of
religious freedom, and the Church's proclamation of the natural law
tradition in the context of modern political life. In addition, one can
also see in the first twenty-two chapters of *Gaudium et spes* a kind of
initial charter for thinking about the Church's missionary outreach
to people from formerly Christian countries affected by modern
agnosticism and atheism, who remain concerned with fundamental questions of meaning, and to whom the Church must cultivate
a new form of intellectual and spiritual mission in the wake of sec-
ularization.

ORDER OF THIS COLLECTION

This set of essays is characterized by a form of conscientious homage to those noteworthy examplars mentioned above. Nevertheless,
it contrasts with them in at least one very important respect. It is
much more deeply marked by a form of continuity with the scholastic Thomistic tradition, both in content and form. In this regard,
the essays in this volume take greater inspiration from a figure like
Alasdair MacIntyre, who has emphasized the capacity of the Thomistic tradition both to maintain classical principles derived from
Aquinas's work and to promote a greater understanding of them
and exploration of them, in dialogical and dialectical engagement
with surrounding, alternative intellectual proposals.[22] In a sense, we
can treat the various authors mentioned above as providing a set
of alternative proposals, in the sense that they each sought in distinct ways to depart from the scholastic form of theology of the

22. See Alasdair MacIntyre, *Three Rival Versions of Moral Inquiry* (Notre Dame, IN:
University of Notre Dame Press, 1990).

pre-conciliar era. They did this, of course, while also translating key acquisitions from that period into new idioms for what they took to be a new epoch.

This set of essays, then, is motivated by a similar set of concerns as those mentioned above, framed in some key respects by the concerns of the Second Vatican Council, even as it also seeks to provide a bridge of continuity back to pre-conciliar forms of theological reasoning based on the Thomistic understanding of principles of Catholic theology and philosophy noted above. The first book contains discussions of the nature of theology in the modern era. The second considers the challenge of the relation of faith and reason in a multi-cultural and secular epoch (including the challenges of materialist atheism and alternative religious traditions). The third book seeks to provide a theocentric, Trinitarian, and Christological vision of theology animated by a reference to Thomistic principles of reflection. The fourth book looks at the mystery of the Church in light of the principles of Christology, seeking to interpret key documents of the Second Vatican Council in a Thomistic fashion. The Church is treated as a primary reference by which one may think about the economy of grace in the world, since all human beings who receive grace and cooperate with it are called implicitly to union with Christ and communion in the Church that is universal, or Catholic. The treatments of Israel and of Mariology are framed in light of ecclesiology, as in the Second Vatican Council document *Lumen gentium*, since the Church issues from the people of Israel, and the Virgin Mary is both the Mother of the Church and her preeminent member.[23] The relations of grace and nature in all human beings are understood in light of this Christological ecclesiology, which depicts the human condition as one that finds its ultimate fulfillment and deepest meaning in the mystery of Christ. Otherwise stated, the internal ordering of the essays present in these books is inspired by the Creed, reread in a contemporary way in part by reference to *Lumen gentium*: the soteriological initiatives of God in the world culminate

23. See *Lumen gentium*, ch. 8.

in Christ and are realized in the Church. All human beings affected by God's grace are mysteriously oriented toward an ecclesial realization of existence. The Church is first then in God's order of intention for the redemption of creation, which is conducted by means of the Incarnation, and the Virgin Mary is the exemplar of ecclesial identity. The order passes from consideration of God as Trinity, to Christ in whom God is manifest, to the Church (which presupposes Israel as foundation and the Virgin Mary as the summit), to the universality of the activity of grace.

One might object that the order of essays in this collection of books runs contrary to that order of Aquinas's we mentioned above, who treats theology according to the order of the principles of the Creed. However, the purpose of this collection of essays is not to repeat materially the content of Aquinas's own theological reflections. Those reflections on the principles of Catholicism are presupposed, not transcended, while these essays seek to make use of those principles within a new theological context, one in which the mystery of the Church in the modern world is of central concern. As such, this collection seeks to treat topics of central interest to the theological guild of our own epoch, but it does so in an alternative way, inspired by the Thomistic tradition and based on the antecedent reflection of the Common Doctor. As such this set of books seeks to be a collection of *nova et vetera*. At its heart it seeks to refer back to and renew reflection upon the perennial principles of Catholic theology, those that derive from reflection on the mystery of revelation in the Thomistic school, as well as from its philosophical traditions. However, it is also a reflection in view of a well-grounded, living treatment of contemporary topics and questions, one that takes place ideally in view of new intellectual orientations and settlements. Together this two-fold form of reflection, which aims at both deep recovery and plausible innovation, is meant to contribute modestly if truly to the renovation and expansion of a living form of Catholic theology marked in a particular way by the influence of Thomas Aquinas and the intellectual traditions of the Dominican Order.

1

The *Analogia Fidei* in Catholic Theology

Modern Christian dogmatics has been characterized by two rival responses to the theoretical challenges of the Enlightenment era. We might consider these responses as prototypes of modern theology.[1] They can serve as an introduction for thinking about the tasks for a modern re-articulation of classical Catholic theology conducted in light of the traditional doctrine of the *analogia fidei*.

Friedrich Schleiermacher and Karl Rahner

On the one side, there is the emergence of modern dogmatics as essentially an outgrowth of "theological anthropology," an idea instantiated in archetypal form by the work of Friedrich Schleiermacher.[2] In the wake of Kant's critique of classical metaphysics and his overt rejection of the intelligibility of Chalcedonian Christology, Schleiermacher developed a distinctly modern alternative to pre-Kantian

---

1. I am partially indebted for this analysis to lectures of John Webster. He in turn was influenced in part I think by Hans Frei, *Types of Christian Theology*, ed. G. Hunsinger and W. C. Placher (New Haven: Yale University Press, 1992).

2. Friedrich Schleiermacher, *The Christian Faith*, 2 vols., ed. H. R. Mackintosh and J. S. Stewart (New York: Harper and Row, 1963). I make this argument at greater length in T. J. White, *The Incarnate Lord: A Thomistic Study in Christology* (Washington, DC: The Catholic University of America Press, 2015), prolegomenon.

Christianity.[3] The starting point is anthropological: every human being is characterized by the search for religious experience of the absolute, and these experiences are thematized conceptually in culturally diverse ways throughout history.[4] Jesus of Nazareth and the religious movement that took inspiration from his example represent the highest, most ethically developed form of religious consciousness in human history, one in which God united humanity to himself in a definitive way.[5] Christianity is the deepest manifestation in history of man's religious response to the absolute and by this very fact is the ultimate expression of the self-communication of God to humanity in history.[6] Traditional doctrines regarding the Trinity, the hypostatic union, atonement, grace, and original sin are conceptual theologoumena: edifying but ultimately gratuitous and artificial superstructures developed out of the anthropological experience of early Christianity.[7] Modern historical and theological study of the New Testament allows us to retrieve the inner spirit of Christianity as a religious and ethical movement prior to its later transformation into a system of abstract dogma and law. Jesus is the absolute religious example who emerges from the evolutionary history of human religion, one given to modern human beings so they might understand their lives ethically against the backdrop of the conceptually unthematizable mystery of God.

Particularly revelatory is Schleiermacher's treatment of the Holy Trinity, which forms a kind of appendix to his dogmatics in *The Christian Faith*.[8] He notes there that the language of the Sonship of Christ and that of the Holy Spirit denote respectively the unity of God with the man Jesus and the unity of God with the communi-

---

3. Immanuel Kant, *The Critique of Pure Reason*, trans. Norman Kemp Smith (New York: Macmillan, 1965); Immanuel Kant, *Religion within the Boundaries of Mere Reason*, trans. A. Wood and G. di Giovanni (Cambridge: Cambridge University Press, 1998).

4. Schleiermacher, *The Christian Faith* I, §§4–10, pp. 12–52.

5. Schleiermacher, *The Christian Faith* II, §94, pp. 385–89.

6. Schleiermacher, *The Christian Faith* I, §§11–14, pp. 52–76; II, §106, pp. 476–78.

7. See, for example, Schleiermacher, *The Christian Faith* I, §§70–72, pp. 282–304; II, §§93–99, pp. 377–424; §§117–20, pp. 536–60; §§160–62, pp. 707–13; §§170–72, pp. 738–51.

8. Schleiermacher, *The Christian Faith* II, §§170–72, pp. 738–51.

ty of the Church.[9] The terms "Son" and "Spirit" denote that the true
and living God, the Father, has truly communicated who he is to
the Church in the person of Christ and in the life of the Spirit in the
Church. Arianism is to be avoided insofar as the Son is he who has
an authentic consciousness of God and communicates to us in turn
authentic knowledge of who God is in himself. So likewise, Sabellianism is to be eschewed insofar as that heresy suggests that the revelation of God as three persons is not adequate to what God really
is in himself, while in fact we come to know God in himself in truth,
by virtue of the Christian mystery.[10] Consequently, the distinction
of Father, Jesus-Son, and the Holy Spirit in the Church, must be in
some way essential to the confession of faith of Christians. We only
ever know God in an economic fashion in history:

We have only to do with the God-consciousness given in our self-con-
sciousness along with our consciousness of the world; hence we have no
formula for the being of God in Himself as distinct from the being of God
in the world, and we should have to borrow any such formula from specu-

9. Schleiermacher, *The Christian Faith* II, §170, pp. 738–39:

An essential element of our exposition in this Part has been the doctrine of
the union of the Divine Essence with human nature, both in the personality
of Christ and in the common Spirit of the Church; therewith the whole view
of Christianity set forth in our Church teaching stands and falls. For unless
the being of God in Christ is assumed, the idea of redemption could not be
thus concentrated in his Person. And unless there were such a union also in the
common Spirit of the Church, the Church could not thus be the Bearer and
Perpetuator of the redemption through Christ.... But at this point we would
call a halt; we cannot attach the same value to the further elaboration of the
dogma, which alone justifies the ordinary term. For the term "Trinity" is really
based on the fact that each of the two above-mentioned unions is traced back
to a separate distinction posited independently of such union, and eternally, in
the Supreme Being as such; further, after the member of this plurality destined
to union with Jesus had been designated by the name "Son," it was felt necessary to posit the Father in accordance therewith as a special distinction. The
result was the familiar dualism-unity of Essence and trinity of Persons. But the
assumption of an eternal distinction in the Supreme Being is not an utterance
concerning the religious consciousness, for there it could never emerge. Who
would venture to say that the impression made by the divine in Christ obliges
us to conceive such an eternal distinction as its basis?

10. Schleiermacher, *The Christian Faith* II, §172, p. 750.

lation and so prove ourselves disloyal to the character of the discipline at which we are working.[11]

That discipline is one in which the self-imposed limitations of post-Kantian reason transpose pre-modern appeals to knowledge of transcendent reality into a transcendental illusion and a mere construct of reason. Consequently, when confronted with the question of the eternal pre-existent Holy Trinity as a mystery characterized by a real distinction of persons, Schleiermacher shows thorough reserve and offers instead a series of supposedly irresolvable conceptual antinomies that he thinks arise from the affirmation of three persons who are one in being.[12] Having implied that the Trinity is literally theologically inconceivable, he suggests that *either* God can only ever be known historically and economically, *or* some kind of Sabellianism must be reconsidered as permissible, so that consequently the doctrine of the Trinity as a truth about God in three persons must be considered a mere theologoumenon or optional speculation of Christian theological reasoning.

Catholic parallels are found in the theology of Karl Rahner.[13] At the heart of his theological project is a universal affirmation regarding theological anthropology: each human being lives out his anthropological condition in concrete history under the effects of the 'supernatural existential' dynamism of grace.[14] This latent dynamism is present in all of human history inviting human beings to interpret their lives against a religious horizon of meaning.[15] It comes to its fruition or perfection historically in Jesus of Nazareth, who is

11. Schleiermacher, *The Christian Faith* II, §172, p. 748.

12. Schleiermacher, *The Christian Faith* II, §171, pp. 742–47.

13. My interpretation of Rahner is influenced by precedent criticisms, including Hans Urs von Balthasar, *The Moment of Christian Witness* (*Cordula oder der Ernstfall*), trans. R. Beckley (San Francisco: Ignatius Press, 1994); Cornelio Fabro, *La svolta antropologica di Karl Rahner*, *Opere Complete* 25 (Rome: EDIVI Press, 2011); Bruce D. Marshall, *Christology in Conflict: The Identity of a Savior in Rahner and Barth* (Oxford: Blackwell, 1987).

14. Karl Rahner, *Foundations of Christian Faith: An Introduction to the Idea of Christianity*, trans. W. Dych (New York: Crossroad, 1978), 126–33.

15. Rahner, *Foundations of Christian Faith*, 138–75.

simultaneously the fulfillment of the universal human religious response to the mystery of God, under the inspiration of grace, and the absolute manifestation of God in history.[16] Rahner's theology of the hypostatic union depicts Jesus of Nazareth both as the eternal Word of God manifest in history and as the perfect embodiment in history of man's *a priori* subjective-transcendental orientation toward God.[17] These two ideas are connected to one another both logically and metaphysically. Jesus of Nazareth shared in a common human history of grace with us, in which he alone was so deeply influenced by grace as to be perfectly turned toward the Father in all of his human knowledge and agency. In virtue of this same perfect awareness and agency of the man Jesus, we see the Logos of the Father shining through his human nature in our shared historical life.

Despite significant differences between Rahner and Schleiermacher, the parallels are important and have yet to be studied in great enough detail. Both work from the premise of a post-Kantian transcendental anthropology and define theology primarily against the backdrop of what they take to be a world history of the religious spirit in humanity, which evolves in diverse ways. Both take grace and nature to be co-extensive in history and to unfold especially though not exclusively in the advent of the religious activity of man. For each the religious consciousness of Christ is the primary locus of the union of God and humanity. The Church is the place where human beings, under the movement of the Holy Spirit, manifest the ongoing union of God and humanity that follows from Christ's example and that approaches asymptotically the perfection of union with God established in Christ. Each of them sees Christianity as the perfection of human religion and stipulates that the self-communication of God in history and the religious self-actualization of humanity are in some way identical processes in reality. Rahner is thoroughly sacramental in his thinking (where Schleiermacher is not) but in a

---

16. Rahner, *Foundations of Christian Faith*, 176–212.

17. Rahner, *Foundations of Christian Faith*, 212–28. I have proposed a critical interpretation of the ontology in Rahner's mature Christology in White, *The Incarnate Lord*, ch. 1.

way that suggests a departure from the Tridentine understanding of sacramentality in noteworthy ways.[18] Rahner affirms unambiguously the historical and physical resurrection of Christ, a commitment that Schleiermacher seems to wish to evade.[19] Rahner is committed to a form of theological reflection that works from within the magisterium of the visible Catholic Church (including frequent and carefully placed references to Denzinger). Schleiermacher typically cites the Lutheran confessions prior to offering his radical reinterpretations of them. Perhaps then they converge and diverge simultaneously on this final point.

Karl Barth and Hans Urs von Balthasar

In juxtaposition to this version of modern theology, one can consider the project of Karl Barth as an archetypal example of holistic "Christological ontology" that aspires to be uniformly theological in kind. Barth famously contests the viability of any and every form of philosophical analysis (modern or ancient) that might lead to a natural knowledge of God.[20] Correspondingly, he also refuses to ground theology in the modern Protestant vision of man as an inherently religious being. Both scholastic metaphysical arguments and post-Kantian anthropology are rejected as foundations upon which to construct a dogmatic science.[21] Therefore, the theological anthropologies of both Schleiermacher and Rahner are excluded methodologically for Christological reasons.[22] Instead, the object of

18. Rahner, *Foundations of Christian Faith*, 411–30. See likewise Karl Rahner, *The Church and the Sacraments*, trans. W. J. O'Hara (New York: Herder and Herder, 1963). I take both Rahner's theory of sacramental efficacy in general and of the Eucharistic presence of Christ in this latter work to be deeply problematic as formulations of Catholic theology.

19. Rahner, *Foundations of Christian Faith*, 245–46, 274–80. For Schleiermacher, see *The Christian Faith* II, §99, pp. 417–21.

20. Including in his late work, see Karl Barth, *Church Dogmatics* IV/3.1, 88–89 (from *Church Dogmatics*, 4 vols. in 13 pts., ed. G. W. Bromiley and T. F. Torrance [Edinburgh: T&T Clark, 1936–75], cited hereafter as *CD*). See Keith Johnson, *Karl Barth and the Analogia Entis* (London: T&T Clark, 2011).

21. Barth, *CD* I/1, 41–42, 280.

22. As an aside, one might consider with interest the letter of Barth to Rahner in 1968 in which he compares the latter's radio addresses to the theology of liberal Protestantism:

theological science must be identified uniquely through a consideration of biblical revelation, centered upon the person and event of Jesus Christ in human history.

Barth affirms that Christ is essentially God and essentially man, and he is the key to understanding rightly the created intelligibility and ultimate meaning of all that exists.[23] We might say, to employ a term from Aquinas, that what follows from this starting point is that *sacra doctrina* (the scientific study of divine revelation) becomes the unique explanatory science of being.[24] This Christ-centered method for understanding reality in general (always with reference to New Testament revelation) is essential for every part of dogmatic reflection but also determinative for any normative account of creaturely ontology. It is theology that provides the universal science of being in Barth's thought, not the medieval study of the transcendentals or metaphysics as "first philosophy."

At the same time, Christ is understood not only by recourse to pre-modern dogmatic traditions, but also simultaneously in distinctly modern ways, by making theological use of concepts from modern German idealist ontologies.[25] One may argue about whether Barth's

---

In the way you are speaking now, so some fifty years ago Troeltsch was speaking of the future of the church and theology ... our Neo-Protestants [like Schleiermacher] were and are in their own way pious ... but with such addresses as you gave on Sunday, which lack spiritual salt ... you are not building up the church in time and on earth ... nor building up the "church for the world." In Karl Barth, *Letters 1961–1968*, trans. G. W. Bromiley (Grand Rapids, MI: Eerdmans, 1981), 278–88.

23. Barth, *CD* IV/2, 47–60, 84–85, 108–15.

24. I am thinking here, for example, of Barth's intendedly thematic Christological rereading of the traditional divine attributes in *CD* II/1, of election in *CD* II/2, and of the ontology of creation and of the human person in *CD* III/1–3.

25. This is particularly clear in Barth's event ontology present in *CD* II/1–2 and IV/1–2 in a variety of places. To give one example, consider *CD* IV/1, 215, regarding the cry of dereliction:

[I]n this event God allows the world and humanity to take part in the history of the inner life of His Godhead, in the movement in which from and to all eternity He is Father, Son and Holy Spirit, and therefore the one true God. But this participation of the world in the being of God implies necessarily His participating in the being of the world, and therefore that His being, His history, is played out as world-history and therefore under the affliction and peril of all world-history. The self-humiliation of God in His Son would not really lead

theological ontology has more in common with his pre-modern forebears or his modern interlocutors. His ontology of God as tri-une, of Christ, and of creation does appeal to an event ontology, in the sense that the being in act of God is itself dynamic and is charac-terized by self-actuation in and through the historical enactment of the Incarnation and the redemption.[26]

Catholic parallels are to be found in the theology of Hans Urs von Balthasar, whose theological studies of the transcendentals (beauty, goodness, and truth) are centered on the mystery and on-tology of Christ, God who has become human. In distinction to Rahner, von Balthasar underscores the importance of classical meta-physics, and in distinction to Barth, he affirms the relative integrity of philosophy as a form of thinking distinct from theological reflec-tion.[27] At the same time, he also perceives the mystery of God's in-carnation, death, and "descent into hell" to be the ultimate epipha-ny of Trinitarian being, as well as the central key to understanding human existence, freedom, and love.[28] Attempts to attain profound

Him to us, the activity in which we see His true deity and the divine Sonship of Jesus Christ would not be genuine and actual, if there were any reservation in respect of His solidarity with us, of His entry into world-history. He did be-come ... the brother of man ... with him in the stream which hurries down-wards to the abyss ... to the cessation of being and nothingness. With him He cries ... "My God. My God, why have you abandoned me?" (Mk 15:34). *Deus pro nobis* means simply that God has not abandoned the world ... that He took it upon Himself, and that He cries with man in this need.

26. CD IV/2 has very strong formulations that tend in a Hegelian direction at times, as does CD II/2. Consider CD IV/2, 84–85, 108–15. Speaking of the Incarnation as God's self-communication to humanity in CD IV/2, 84, Barth states:

We must begin with the fact that what takes place in this address is also and primarily a determination of divine essence: not an alteration, but a determi-nation. God does not first elect and determine man but Himself. In His eternal counsel, and then in its execution in time He determines to address Himself to man, and to do so in such a way that He Himself becomes man. God elects and determines Himself to be the God of man. And this undoubtedly means ... that He elects and determines Himself for humiliation.

27. See, for example, von Balthasar, *The Moment of Christian Witness*, 59–76; Hans Urs von Balthasar, *The Theology of Karl Barth: Exposition and Interpretation*, trans. E. Oakes (San Francisco: Ignatius Press, 1992), 302–25.

28. This is said with exquisite clarity in Hans Urs von Balthasar, *Epilogue*, trans.

knowledge of reality by means of pre-Christian forms of reflection are only ever anticipatory adumbrations of the ontology of the Trinity, the Incarnation, and of Christ's dereliction on the Cross. Faith leads the Catholic metaphysician across the divided line, into the deepest creases of being.[29] Seemingly non-Christian forms of knowledge are seen retrospectively as temporal moments (like musical movements) within a larger 'symphony' of knowledge centered on Christ and expressive of the mystery of the Holy Trinity. All things take on their final intelligibility only in light of the unity and distinction of divine and human essences in Jesus, particularly as the event of his being human and divine itself unfolds and is manifest in his Paschal mystery.[30] The outward historical event of the crucifixion and dereliction are expressive of the inward eternal transcendent structure of the Trinitarian persons as characterized by eternal freedom, self-emptying kenosis, and love.[31]

Critical Concerns

Both Schleiermacher and Barth have inheritors in the postmodern theological context. Theological anthropologies in the early twenty-first century tend to become liberation theologies, theologies of the politics of identity, or theologies of religious pluralism. The reasons

---

E. Oakes (San Francisco: Ignatius Press, 2004), 89–98, where von Balthasar is summarizing his theological project.

29. See Hans Urs von Balthasar, *Theo-Logic: Theological Logical Theory*, vol. 2, *The Truth of God*, trans. A. Walker (San Francisco: Ignatius Press, 2004), 173–218.

30. Von Balthasar, *Epilogue*, 23–39.

31. Von Balthasar, *Epilogue*, 89–90:

How can Jesus say of himself, "I am the Truth"? This is possible only because all that is true in the world "hold[s] together" in him (Col 1:17), which in turn presupposes that the *analogia entis* is personified in him, that he is the adequate sign, surrender, and expression of God within finite being. To approach this mystery we must try to think: In God himself the total epiphany, self-surrender, and self-expression of God the Father *is* the Son, identical with him as God, in whom everything—even everything that is possible for God—is expressed. Only if God freely decides in the Son to bring forth a fullness of nondivine beings can the Son's essentially 'relative' and thus 'kenotic' act in God be seen as a personal act (*esse completum subsistens*) within the act of creation that gives to everything its real identity (*esse completum sed non subsistens*).

are simple: as the ethical conventions of modern culture change, the anthropological locus of theology must change as well. Barth's and von Balthasar's great Christological visions have inspired projects of postmodernity that are philosophically anti-foundationalist, denying the basis for definitive knowledge of God or of ultimate human purposes stemming from secular university disciplines. All true wisdom in an epistemologically disoriented modernity originates in primal fashion from divine revelation. These projects seek to retrieve facets of traditional Christian doctrine, ontology, and ethics so as to present them anew in a secular context, based on appeal to divine revelation, typically in critical comparison with modern and postmodern European philosophies. These two rival versions of theology characterize much of what constitutes academic theology in our era.

There are intellectual difficulties that arise within each of these modern traditions, which they each share despite their historical stances of opposition to one another. Neither Schleiermacher nor Barth (geniuses though they unquestionably were) adequately challenged at a sufficiently radical level the intellectually questionable Kantian consensus of their age. Like their contemporaries, they presupposed the death of metaphysics too prematurely and in too arbitrary a fashion. At the same time, they also each embraced philosophical modes of reflection emergent from nineteenth-century German philosophy in a theologically self-conscious way. But they did so without submitting these theological choices to sufficient philosophical scrutiny. A theology of revelation wed inextricably to an errant ontology or theological anthropology becomes an implausible form of theological thinking, since grace does not destroy nature but presupposes it and is meant to heal it over time. There is no surrogate for for a defective nature. Theological truth cannot be expressed effectively except by making use of a balanced, realistic philosophy. This is precisely why a perennial philosophical tradition of wisdom (both before and after the modern era) must continue to accompany theology and must be maintained within the Church in her reflection on divine revelation. Such a "perennial" philosophy is not only influential within theology but is influenced continuously by a sufficient engagement with the truths of divine revelation, so that it is purified by the distinctive influences of grace dialectically through the intellectual history of the Church.

In the absence of a sufficiently ecclesial discernment on this front, the theologies of both rival versions mentioned above suffer from a lack of critical engagement with the classical patrimony of the Church's scriptural and doctrinal tradition.[32] Both doctrines and theological traditions that come from before the decisive epoch of post-Kantian modernity are subject to radical revision. The truths of the Catholic faith articulated by the great tradition are now deemed inaccessible or inherently unintelligible. This includes those regarding God (the Holy Trinity especially characterized in terms of the psychological analogy, the divine essence including the attributes of divine simplicity, immutability, omnipotence and omniscience), creation (participation metaphysics, primary and secondary causality), human beings (the spiritual soul and the hylomorphic constitution of the human person), sacraments (sacramental causality, the ontology of the Eucharist), and ethics (the teleological orientation of the human person, the ontology of created grace, the structure of the infused theological virtues). Consequently, key elements of doctrine that stem originally from the New Testament revelation must be abandoned or ignored.

This rupture of methodological unity of theology and classical philosophy in turn impeded the modern traditions in their capacity to think theoretically about the conditions of *sacra doctrina* within a modern context, as a form of reflection that must make inevitable use of the "lesser sciences" of metaphysics, philosophy of nature, philosophical anthropology, and philosophical ethics, subordinate

---

32. Evidently von Balthasar is an exception here, who could hardly be accused of failing to engage with the pre-modern Catholic tradition. Much of his theology is an effort especially to do precisely that. However, in the comments that follow and that are of a more general nature, I am presuming that von Balthasar, despite the riches of his thought, did often fail to preserve (and in fact purposefully abandoned) key elements of the tradition that are in critical need of retention.

to and within the context of a distinctively Christian theological form of thinking about divine revelation as such.

Consequently, neither of these modern traditions provided a sufficient form of thinking to engage intellectually with the challenges of the modern sciences (modern cosmology, evolutionary theory, neuroscience), nor a way to formulate a mature vision of the human being as made in the image of God, within the context of the modern scientific ethos. In fact, it should be noted in no uncertain terms that in the twentieth century there was an absence of serious engagement with the modern sciences among the major theologians (with the possible exceptions of Wolfhart Pannenberg and Thomas F. Torrance).[33] Nor were either of these traditions able to engage adequately with the emergent field of comparative religious studies, so as to consider Christianity in comparison to non-Christian religions according to its various similitudes and its irreducible uniqueness. For this a deeper analysis of human religiosity would be required, one that is simultaneously informed by divine revelation and by an adequate metaphysical reflection and philosophical anthropology.

Again, due to an absence of docile reception of the Christian scholastic tradition, these traditions have been unable to articulate a thoroughgoing Christian ethics based on a realistic analysis of human action, virtue theory, human purposes (teleology), and a comprehensive, nuanced theory of the cardinal virtues in relation to the infused theological virtues. This lack of Aristotelianism is coupled with an ignorance of the nuanced Augustinianism developed by the scholastic heritage, presented for example by the treatment of the effects of original sin, the need for grace, the role of the commandments, and the centrality of the virtues as depicted archetypally by the Roman Catechism derived from the Council of Trent. As a result, the political theologies of modernity that have emerged from within a post-Kantian, post-Hegelian ambit tend to be unmoored from any sufficient reference to the perennial structure of human

---

33. See, in particular, Wolfhart Pannenberg, *Theology and the Philosophy of Science*, trans. F. McDonagh (Philadelphia: Westminster John Knox Press, 1976).

nature, its realistic possibilities under grace, and its fallen character. What typically emerges instead is a historicist view of human ethics, often utopian, whether of the Marxist variant or as derived from Hegelian liberalism. These latter trends often concoct a distinctively modern form of Pelagianism that stems from Kant's anthropology and moral theory, in which human beings can right themselves and their social constitution over time by the moral use of their individual free will. True Christian theology cannot be built upon this crumbling edifice.

THE *ANALOGIA FIDEI* AND THE *ANALOGIA ENTIS* IN MODERN CATHOLIC THEOLOGY

Among theologians in the twentieth century, it was Gottlieb Söhngen above all who was able to state clearly and in the most nuanced terms the conditions for a genuine restatement of Catholic theology within a modern context.[34] Erich Przywara had sought in his studies on the *analogia entis* to think out a comprehensive response of the Catholic intellectual tradition to the emergence of secular modernity.[35] His attempt at a historical retrieval of Aquinas's metaphysics was coupled with a profound engagement with modern German philosophy, Hegel, Husserl, and Heidegger in particular. His metaphysical analysis of the dynamic structure and 'rhythm' of created being attempted to show how natural created reality is itself always already open to a completion 'from above' that comes to creatures in virtue of God's supernatural grace, as a gift that is simultaneously gratuitous and that also elevates and fulfills the deepest impulses and dynamisms of created nature. The similitude between God and

34. See, in particular, Gottlieb Söhngen, "The Analogy of Faith: Likeness to God from Faith Alone?," trans. K. Oakes, *Pro Ecclesia* 21 (2012): 56–76, and Gottlieb Söhngen, "The Analogy of Faith: Unity in the Science of Faith," trans. K. Oakes, *Pro Ecclesia* 21 (2012): 169–94. The originals appeared in the German theology journal *Catholica* in 1934.

35. See the helpful analysis by John Betz, "Beyond the Sublime: The Aesthetics of the Analogy of Being," *Modern Theology* 21 (2005): 367–411, and *Modern Theology* 22 (2006): 1–50.

creatures (and the ever-greater dissimilitude between them) is not dissolved by the Incarnation or by divine revelation but is recapitulated in supernatural terms. In the revelation of the Holy Trinity given to us in Christ, we perceive a greater likeness between humanity and God than we have ever perceived or could perceive in the natural structure of creation. And we also perceive a greater dissimilitude, in the sense that the transcendence and alterity of God as wholly other than creation is made manifest to us in the most profound way due precisely to God's wholly new and unexpected presence to creation in Christ.[36]

Karl Barth perceived in this structure of thinking what he took to be a form of epistemological works-righteousness (an invention of the anti-Christ), in which fallen human beings seek to lay hold of the conditions of God's revelation and control artificially the conditions of its interpretation, based on alien philosophical speculation and the ecclesiological-institutional apparatus of the Roman Church. However, Barth was deeply influenced by the challenge of Przywara's way of thinking and undoubtedly impressed by the breadth and ambition of his Catholic intellectual perspective. He developed as an alternative in his *Church Dogmatics* a theology of the so-called *analogia fidei*: there is a similitude and dissimilitude between God and creatures discernable only in the revelation given in Jesus Christ and accessible to us in virtue of the apostolic testimony presented in sacred Scripture. This perspective is consistent with Barth's own theological ontology, in which he sought to engage many of the same modern sources and questions as Przywara but from within what he took to be a uniquely theological point of view.

Both approaches present difficulties, as Söhngen rightly saw, and neither of them convey precisely what the classical theological tra-

36. See the intriguing expression of this idea in Erich Przywara, *Analogia Entis: Metaphysics: Original Structure and Universal Rhythm*, trans. J. Betz and D. B. Hart (Grand Rapids, MI: Eerdmans, 2014), Part II, ch. 2, "The Scope of Analogy as a Fundamental Catholic Form," 348–99. Przywara strongly contrasts his own position with that of Söhngen on p. 397. I agree that their positions are distinct but disagree with Przywara's characterization, which problematically assimilates Söhngen's positions to those of Barth.

dition took to be the sense of the terms *analogia entis* and *analogia fidei*.[37] Przywara sought to show how a realistic metaphysical understanding of the created order coordinates deeply with a theological analysis of the mystery of divine revelation and redemption. However, he includes theological revelation within the ambit of the 'analogy of being' as a kind of extension of philosophical knowledge. By casting his approach to revealed mysteries of the Catholic faith in terms of the analogy of being, he created an inevitable ambiguity.[38] His thought can be read as an immense project of theological ontology (similar to that of Barth) in which the mysteries of the faith presuppose and in fact give formal determination to our interpretation of metaphysics.[39] Or it can be read as an immense project of metaphysics and anthropology that organically opens upwards toward the mysteries of revelation, grace, and incarnation, so that the latter are expressions of the former.[40] This distinction-within-unity of nature and grace, faith and natural reason has an integral unity that is theoretically admirable but theologically ambiguous.

Barth wondered how an ontology of being as such could serve as the foundation for sacred theology. However, Barth's reaction is a dialectical, mirror-opposite vision, marked by many of the same ambiguities. His is a theology of the Incarnation and redemption, the knowledge made possible by revelation, created being revealed in Christ and human nature made transparent in Christ. Here, then, the vision of ontology is provided entirely 'from the top downwards' through divine revelation and the manifestation of the *analogia fidei* in Christ alone. If the *analogia entis* is too ambitiously theological and not sufficiently distinctly metaphysical for Przywara, the

37. Consider the alternative presentation of Söhngen, "The Analogy of Faith: Unity in the Science of Faith," 169–70.
38. As von Balthasar saw. See his clearly critical remarks in *Theo-Logic II: The Truth of God*, 94–95n16, and the logically congruent remarks on 273n109.
39. As in the interpretation of Kenneth Oakes, "The Cross and the *Analogia Entis* in Erich Przywara," in T. J. White, ed., *The Analogy of Being: Invention of the Antichrist or the Wisdom of God?* (Grand Rapids, MI: Eerdmans, 2011), 147–71.
40. As in the interpretation of Richard Schenk, "Analogy as the *discrimen naturae et gratiae*: Thomism and Ecumenical Learning," in White, *The Analogy of Being*, 172–91.

analogia fidei is too ambitiously metaphysical for Barth, and not sufficiently Christological as such, that is to say, distinctively theological
in kind. Barth thinks the very opposite, of course, but his uncritical
or sometimes quite questionable assimilation of modern German-
ic (or pre-modern classical) ontological motifs into his Christology
is not in reality based upon his commitment to the New Testament
but upon his post-Kantian, post-Hegelian philosophical proclivities,
which remain unacknowledged and therefore insufficiently rationally warranted, even at the risk of methodical incoherence. That is to
say, I take it that Barth never makes *uniquely* theological arguments.
Instead, he makes nuanced and sustained use of modern philosophical ideas within his theology, even while claiming to act in a methodologically homogeneous way, so as to conduct a reflection on divine
revelation alone. It is unclear if one who conducts himself in this
way is permitted ever to acknowledge his philosophical and modern
scientific influences, distinctively philosophical questions about the
truth content of non-Christian religions, or his conclusions of sound
philosophical reasoning, insofar as they have any distinct epistemic
warrant and integrity in logical articulation as such.

The irony of this form of thought is that while it seeks to provide
a holistic account of Christian doctrine in a modern context, it in
fact remains so methodologically extrinsic to the natural intellectual
disciplines it seeks to integrate, and to metaphysically realist philosophy in particular, that it must necessarily be incapable of integrating
the truths and conclusions of non-Christian disciplines into itself in
a warranted, coherent, and objective fashion. This difficulty that arises from the method of Christological extrinsicism is a price Barth
needs to pay to preserve what he takes theology to be as an autonomous science.[41] It is an unwarranted decision, however, and one that
ironically risks sacrificing genuine theological science entirely, even
while being based on the motive of saving it. It impedes a genuine
Christo-centricism, in which all truths are assimilated in an organic

41. Barth says as much in *CD* I/1, 5–13, 41–42, 223–27, 275–87.

way to the uniquely saving truth about God revealed in Christ and to the revelation of the New Testament.

In contradistinction to the tendencies of thought bequeathed to us by the Przywara-Barth debate, what may be presupposed in Catholic theology are two distinct subjects: (1) the articulation of a metaphysical understanding of natural reality that is compatible with divine revelation but not identical with the revelation of Christ, and (2) an understanding of revelation that is scientific in kind (according to the classical Catholic understanding of *sacra doctrina* and the *analogia fidei*), but one that does not seek to replace a realistic philosophical metaphysics and a philosophical study of the natural world with an epistemological monism governed exclusively by the judgments of faith. A balanced, Catholic form of theological reflection is respectful and assimilative of all natural learning, including the philosophical wisdom of the *analogia entis*, while also testing and formulating the latter in the light of the revelation of God in the life of Jesus Christ, so as to measure the fallible human judgments of the philosophers in the light of the Trinity, and the Incarnation, Cross, and resurrection of the Incarnate Son.[42] For this reason, classical Catholic theology is capable of assimilating all genuine natural truths of human understanding into a deeper Christological form of wisdom, a science of God the Holy Trinity made possible uniquely in virtue of the revelation given to Israel and brought to fulfillment in Christ and the Church. Far from being hindered by the distinction between supernatural faith and metaphysical realism, this form of thinking distinguishes the two sources of knowledge in order to unite them.[43] The distinct forms of knowledge that derive from the *analogia fidei* and the *analogia entis* can be coordinated and integrated without destroying any genuine insight that stems either from the mystery of the Logos incarnate, crucified, and resurrected, or the patrimony of human philosophical, scientific, and religious learning. Such thinking is authentically Christocentric and universal or 'Cath-

---

42. See Aquinas, *ST* I, q. 1, a. 5 and a. 6, corp. and ad 2 and 3.
43. See in this respect the teaching of the First Vatican Council, *Dei Filius* (1870).

olic' thought, precisely because it is able to unite supernatural and natural truths while maintaining their distinction, harmony, and mutual integration.

Söhngen sought to restate the terms of the dispute about the *analogia fidei* and the *analogia entis* in this sense, with reference to a deeper grounding in traditional sources but also in response to the challenge of the modern secular ethos both Przywara and Barth were concerned to engage with. He noted that in nineteenth-century and early-twentieth-century Catholic theology the term *analogia fidei* was employed in magisterial documents of the Catholic Church to denote at least four distinct but interrelated notions: (1) the unity of Scripture and the senses of Scripture, (2) the unity of the words of Scripture and Church proclamation, (3) the unity and the enigmatic coherence of the mysteries of faith, and (4) the unity of nature and natural knowing with the obedience of grace and faith. Let us consider each of these notions briefly in turn.[44]

The First Sense of the *Analogia Fidei:* Unity of Scripture and the Senses of Scripture

The traditional Catholic use of the term 'analogy of faith' is grounded in the idea of the connectedness of all revealed truth.[45] The fundamental connection of likeness and dissimilarity between the mysteries of faith is ontological in kind. There are diverse mysteries of

44. Particularly in the second essay: Söhngen, "The Analogy of Faith: Unity in the Science of Faith."

45. Söhngen, "The Analogy of Faith: Unity in the Science of Faith," 170, appeals in particular to *Dei Filius*, ch. 4, which reads:

> And, indeed, reason illustrated by faith, when it zealously, piously, and soberly seeks, attains with the help of God some understanding of the mysteries, and that a most profitable one, not only from the analogy of those things which it knows naturally, but also from the connection of the mysteries among themselves and with the last end of man; nevertheless, it is never capable of perceiving those mysteries in the way it does the truths which constitute its own proper object.

Likewise, the 1994 *Catechism of the Catholic Church*, §114, states in succinct fashion: "By 'analogy of faith' we mean the coherence of the truths of faith among themselves and within the whole plan of Revelation."

the Christian religion: the mystery of the Holy Trinity, the Incarnation, the atonement, the resurrection, the sanctity and spiritual communion of the Catholic Church, the seven sacraments, and so forth. The fundamental mysteries of the Catholic religion are concerned with God himself: the Holy Trinity and the Incarnation. Most of the mysteries do not concern God in himself (such as the mystery of Israel or the Church) but are expressive of the wisdom and grace of God the Holy Trinity, and so they bear a resemblance both to God and to one another ontologically. They are also distinct and therefore dissimilar to one another in various respects, and of course they only reveal God partially. In other words, the mysteries come from the same source and reflect that source, as effects resemble their cause. Because this is the case, the teachings of divine revelation that denote these ontological realities are themselves coordinated teachings that give rise to a unified science, a distinct and coherent body of knowledge, in virtue of the fact that they all denote realities that reveal God.[46] All the truths of the Catholic faith are therefore related to one other and help to illumine one another, just as the mysteries they denote are related to one another and serve to illumine one another.[47]

Evidently this truth about divine teaching must have its basis first and foremost in scriptural revelation, where the truth about God is unveiled. Scripture is not like other books, since in and through Scripture, it is God who speaks as from a living source, like the active voice of another person who is turning his face toward us and speaking, sunlight actively shining from the sun itself, or water flowing actively from a living stream. God manifests himself in a determinative and pre-eminent way in the activity of the Word of God: where the Word of God is proclaimed, read, taught, or preached. The Bible is rightly considered one book, even while being composed of a collec-

---

46. As Aquinas notes in *Summa theologiae* II–II, q. 1, by virtue of supernatural faith and through the medium of divine revelation, we truly come to know who God, the first truth, is in himself.

47. The modern arguments of Matthias Scheeben serve as a precedent of Söhngen in this respect.

tion of distinct ancient writings, because the collection in question is inspired by God and in such a way as to speak to the Church, the apostolic community that is continually given the grace to hear and understand the revelation communicated in Scripture.[48]

Consequently, the diverse and multifarious teachings of this book can and rightly should be interpreted in relation to one another, as teaching stemming from the one God, despite or perhaps precisely in and through the various tensions and differentiations present in biblical revelation. The texts of Scripture speak to one another and of one another in a coherent way that stems from within, so as to illumine from within the living identity of God, who manifests himself to the Church especially in the figure of Jesus Christ, who is both God and man and who is perennially alive in virtue of his bodily resurrection and glorification. This Lord who speaks to the Church reveals the Father, from whom he comes forth as one eternally begotten in his glory, and he reveals the Holy Spirit, who proceeds from the Father and himself eternally and whom Christ sends upon the Church. Again, the content of Scripture is that of a public, prophetic revelation expressed in a way that is entirely human, marked in unmistakable ways by a myriad of human historical characteristics, but which is also entirely divine in origin, living in inspiration and purpose. In and through the Scriptures, it is God the Holy Trinity, revealed in Jesus Christ, who speaks to the Catholic Church.[49]

The Catholic theological tradition speaks therefore of diverse senses of Scripture: the literal, moral, typological, and anagogical.[50] The literal sense denotes a reality that Scripture depicts, in whatever analytic, narrative, or symbolic mode. For example, the literal sense of Genesis 1–2 pertains to the physical cosmos as the ontologically ordered creation of God, which he sustains in being, as well as to the

---

48. Söhngen, "The Analogy of Faith: Unity in the Science of Faith," 171: "The Catholic exposition of Scripture also works under the assumption that the Word of God is its own interpreter. Catholic doctrine holds fast to the whole of Scripture because it takes Scripture to be a whole. It assumes that the inner unity of Scripture, which means the unity of its truth, is given in the unity of its primary author, the Holy Spirit."
49. See Second Vatican Council, *Dei Verbum*, §21.
50. See *Catechism of the Catholic Church*, §§113–19.

human being as one who is made in the image of God, as body and soul, male and female. These realities are denoted in symbolic fashion, but creation itself is the reality denoted. The mode of signification is distinct from the thing signified, and it is the latter that is the object of the literal sense.[51] The Song of Songs denotes literally (one could argue) the love that exists between God and Israel, and it does so by a mode of signification that is poetic. The book of Ruth denotes literally (through the medium of an ancient popular story) the origins of the Davidic monarchy, and in doing so it seeks to denote literally as well the mystery of gentile incorporation into the covenant of God with Israel and its soteriological significance. The prologue of John's Gospel denotes literally the transcendent mystery of the eternal Logos of God and his visible manifestation in the Incarnation.

The other senses of Scripture are founded in the literal sense, since they have their basis not primarily in the inspired text per se but in the ontological reality denoted by the text, insofar as that reality itself points toward or indicates a sacred truth or is related ontologically to another reality.[52] The moral sense is found in the ethical exemplarism of the reality denoted. The typological sense is found in the reality insofar as it anticipates the mystery of Christ and the Church (in the Old Testament) or the post-apostolic Church (in the New Testament). For example, the paschal lamb of Exodus 12 is a foreshadowing of the Christ, according to the Gospel of John (1:29), but the exchanges between Christ and the apostles in John 6 and 20–21 are typologies of the life of the later Church. The anagogical sense is found in the reality insofar as it anticipates the eschaton, and the mystery of the life of Christ in glory, in the ecclesial communion of the life to come. According to 1 Peter 3:20, the ark of Noah is a foreshadowing of the Church, but it is also a symbol of the mystery of salvation. Understood in this way, the 'spiritual senses' of Scrip-

51. Aquinas discusses the distinction between the reality signified and the mode of signification in *Summa theologiae* I, q. 13, a. 3, and it can readily be applied to his discussion of the distinct senses of Scripture in *Summa theologiae* I, q. 1, aa. 9–10.
52. Aquinas, *ST* I, q. 1, a. 10.

ture presuppose the ontology of the life of grace as inclined (before the reality of the Incarnation) toward the mystery of Christ or as inclined (after the Incarnation) toward the mystery of the Church as an ontological reality, both in the current state of this world and in view of the eschatological life of the world to come. Significations and literary styles are only secondary and of remote importance for understanding the spiritual senses. The ontology of the Holy Trinity and the mystery of the life of grace is always and everywhere primary.

From this way of reading Scripture there emerges an understanding of the divine economy as the unfolding of God's numinous and sovereign activity within creation, sometimes quite hidden and sometimes amazingly manifest, as the expression of God's own hidden wisdom, within the human race, which is itself a great enigma and mystery, by virtue of Israel in its scandalous and persistent singularity as a chosen people, within Christ as the unique mediator between God and humanity, himself God, and in the mystery of the Church that is marked by the sanctity of Christ even in the midst of human sinfulness, all in view of eschatological ends. In this mystery, all things come from God and return to God, all things follow a pattern of *exitus* and *reditus*, bearing the trace of their derivative emanation from God and marked in their depths by the inclination or anticipation of their return to God.[53] They have their ground and meaning, ultimately, in the mystery of God himself, even as he remains utterly distinct from the world of creation and is hidden by it. The *analogia fidei* emerges in his context as the interconnection of biblical truths and as a principle of interpretation of the scriptural deposit of faith.

In the context of modern culture, the Church's claim that Scripture is truly inspired and that its mysteries are interrelated must inevitably confront a set of valid intellectual concerns. How does the claim that God truly reveals himself in the Scriptures relate to the

53. See on this topic, M. J. Le Guillou, *Christ and Church: A Theology of the Mystery,* trans. C. Schaldenbrand (New York: Desclee, 1966).

human historicity of this text, its manifold authors and editors, within their various cultural situations, especially as these latter situations bear upon the composition and intentions of the original texts of Scripture? Does the human antiquity of the Old and New Testament in virtue of their historical contingency and cultural particularity rule out for good reason the claim that these works may aspire to speak universally to all human beings in all times and places? What role does the natural religious aspiration of human culture play in the formation of these works, and to what extent or in what way might they be explained historically (or not so explained) as 'merely' or as primarily cultural artifacts of the particular religious traditions that gave rise to them? How can they aspire in a reasonable way to give insight into the human condition or the ontological structure of reality in such a way as to denote realistically what is true as such about God, creatures, and humanity, or may they really do so without intellectual pretense or façade? If they do so, how do they relate to other religious traditions and alternative appeals to divine revelation in the history of human religion, and by what kinds of similitudes or dis-similitudes? *In a word, how is the Biblical revelation truly unique and genuinely universal?*

Catholic theology seeks to answer these questions not by way of an exercise that takes place outside of, prior to, or antecedent to a theological treatment of the doctrines of the Church as such, but within and as a dimension of her treatment of the truths of divine revelation. There is a unity in divine revelation by virtue of its origin and its object, since it is given by God and is about God. But this unity is also assimilative of what is human. The revelation is given in time and through the medium of human culture, by human beings, and it is received by and within various structures of human tradition. A sound theological treatment of the *analogia fidei* must allow each of these dimensions of Scripture to emerge simultaneously, since divine revelation is simultaneously divine and human in form, just as Christ is both human and divine.

The Second Sense of the *Analogia Fidei*: The Unity of the Words of Scripture and Church Proclamation

Catholicism is interpellated by the classical Protestant criticism of various Catholic doctrines as theoretical innovations and consequently has to think carefully through the theoretical conditions of its own doctrinal knowledge and its authoritative pronouncements. In this respect, a fundamental concern of modern Catholic theology is to take account of the basic continuity and organic development of Catholic doctrine down through time. Of course, here one may think first and foremost of John Henry Newman's seven criteria for the identification of genuine doctrinal developments in accord with what Joseph Ratzinger terms a hermeneutic of continuity, as contrasted with doctrinal corruptions, ruptures, or innovations.[54] Newman provides a helpful model for the consideration of doctrine in historical terms. At the same time, the modern historicization of theological method brings with it its own risks. Genuine Catholic theology should take account of the ongoing development of doctrine with nuance and historical sensitivity but in such a way as to terminate in speculative considerations, in the exercise of theology as a science about reality, not a mere archeology of the history of ideas or a relativistic collation-by-chronology of disparate theological opinions. Truth be told, the latter trend has been a normative practice in many quarters since the Second Vatican Council and continues to plague the discipline of academic theology, which is overly historicist.

Questions inevitably emerge regarding the Catholic claim to a continuity of teaching down through time and also in view of the eschaton. The Church rightly regards the prophetic teaching of the Old and New Testaments as the font of revelation and considers the knowledge of the apostolic age as the authoritative source and the exclusive measure of all subsequent doctrinal affirmations.[55] But

---

54. See the significant study of this topic by Ian Ker, *Newman on Vatican II* (Oxford: Oxford University Press, 2014).

55. Söhngen, "The Analogy of Faith: Unity in the Science of Faith," 174: "The divine-

how is this possible if the prophets and apostles clearly reflected in less conceptually precise and systematic ways than church doctors and theologians of subsequent eras? What is the relation between the apostolic mediation of revelation and the post-apostolic constitution of ecclesial teaching?[56] Analogously, how ought we to understand the diversity and unity of doctrines elaborated across time and place within the one Catholic Church? Are there cases of radical change and even discontinuity? Are the forms of continuity that emerge always clearly rooted in Scripture and if so, how is this the case? What epistemic responsibility does the modern human person have to seek to uncover the historical roots of doctrine and to what extent is such an aspiration unreasonable and presumptuous given the natural limits of our historical knowledge?

Likewise, how are we to understand the universality of the Church's teaching as she develops over time, both internally in her own life and practice, and doctrinally in her self-expression and intellectual coherence? How does this claim to universality that takes on a historical development differ from or relate to the rival and alternative traditions that claim to offer alternative forms of universal rationality and explanation of reality, be they, for example, those of rival religious traditions (Islam) or issued from the secular ambitions of the Enlightenment (Hegelian-inspired liberalism, or the new possibility in modernity of scientistic atheism)? These too are 'traditions' that aspire to universal intellectual precedence.

How is the Church's claim to historical continuity and institutional stability related to the eschatological orientation of the Church? Can she persist through time, in view of the final state of humanity and the cosmos, in spite of or in and through the various changes of the world, be they material, spiritual, philosophi-

---

apostolic and dogmatic (limited to doctrinal and ethical teaching) tradition can relate to Holy Scripture in three ways: literally agreeing with or depending upon the words of Scripture (*inhaesiva*), preserving or clarifying (*declarativa*), and illuminating or establishing (*constiutiva*)."

56. On these questions, I take the work of both Charles Journet and Yves Congar to be of definitive importance.

cal, or political? If so, what are the ecclesiological presuppositions
of our claim that she can teach "the same truth" even until the last
day and the final hour? This last criterion for thinking about the development of her doctrine touches directly upon the Church's relationship to alternative religious traditions and rival philosophies, as
well as her relationship to modern cosmology and science, antici-
pating the fourth criterion of the *analogia fidei* named by Söhngen,
to which we will return below. How does the Church present anew
in each epoch her own internal rationality, as declaring an ultimate
truth about the world, in light of Christ? These various questions are
noted here not in order to problematize the faith, nor to suggest that
no good answers have been offered. (Many have.) They are listed in
order to suggest that there are many unfinished, pressing tasks that
arise today in Catholic dogmatics. To treat them one would do well
to return to resources from the past and to apply those resources to
the evident challenges that currently arise and greet us in our path.

The Third Sense of the *Analogia Fidei*: Unity and the Enigmatic Coherence of the Mysteries of Faith

The central aim of Catholic theology is the exploration of the *analogia fidei* in this sense. What is the intellectual content of the Nicene
Creed? What are the key or core mysteries of the faith? What nucleus of intelligibility is present in each, and what does each reveal
to us about God? How are the mysteries related to one another and
how do they relate intelligibly?

He who speaks of a "mystery" of the Catholic religion denotes
(a) a reality filled with divine meaning and intelligibility, (b) accessible to our understanding only by virtue of the supernatural grace
of faith, (c) that is revelatory of the identity of God, (d) that has universal significance for all humanity, and (e) that can never be exhaus-
tively understood by means of our theological investigation.

The mysteries of the faith have a unity, a distinctive content or
specificity, and a hierarchy. The unity stems from their fundamental
origin and object, who is God, about which we will have more to say

below. The distinctive content is not enigmatic, because it is depicted clearly in antecedent Catholic tradition. Theology considers the
mystery of God, the creation, spiritual creatures capable of beatitude
(angels and human beings), Israel, law and grace, the Incarnation and
the mysteries of the life of Christ, the Virgin Mary, the Church and
the sacraments, the moral and spiritual life of sanctity, and the eschatological destiny of creation. Formally speaking, this is what theology is concerned with. (And correspondingly, what anyone writes
that does not concern itself with such topics in truth is not theology.[57]) These distinct and interconnected truths are denoted clearly
by the Creed, even if some are designated only in implicit ways. The
hierarchy of the mysteries follows from the hierarchy of being that is
made manifest by the revelation of God. The Holy Trinity is the first
and final truth of divine revelation. The incarnation of the Son and
the sending of the Holy Spirit are the central mysteries of the divine
economy, by which the identity of God is revealed, human beings are
redeemed, and the life of grace is communicated. Among creatures,
spiritual creatures have a place of ontological dignity and of eschatological destiny that is unique because they are made in the image
of God. The Virgin Mary is the mother of God and the mother of
the Church, the pre-eminent member of the communion of saints.
Among the sacraments, the Eucharist has a place of ontological precedence as the real presence of the body and blood of Christ.

The heart of Catholic theology is to acknowledge and analyze
these mysteries in the aim of understanding the intrinsic ontological form of each in its radiance and activity and the relationships
that emerge between them. This study invites human beings to engage with the question of their final end and with the topic of the
teleological hope of the human race, because it places them before
the possibility of eternal salvation or damnation, everlasting beatitude or perpetual misery. In this sense, theology is practical as well

57. I take it that in the nineteenth and twentieth centuries one finds quite diverse,
successful realizations of Catholic theology, in thinkers such as John Henry Newman,
Matthias Josef Scheeben, Réginald Garrigou-Lagrange, Henri de Lubac, Jean-Hervé
Nicolas, Louis Bouyer, Charles Journet, Joseph Ratzinger, and Pope John Paul II.

as speculative. It is not only a form of *scientia* but also of *sapientia*, as we will have occasion to consider below. The analysis of the *analogia fidei* aims at the depiction of why the mysteries exist and toward what end, what humanity might rightly hope for, and those mysteries in which all things culminate.

The Fourth Sense of the *Analogia Fidei*: Unity of Nature and Natural Knowing with the Obedience of Grace and Faith

Our first three considerations gave attention primarily to the *nexus mysteriorum*, the connectedness of the mysteries of faith. The fourth principle is concerned with the connection of the mysteries to the *analogia entis*. Catholic theology must seek to underscore the harmony of divine revelation and natural human reason, and acknowledge faith's deep unity with reason without dissolving the distinct orders of natural and supernatural knowledge so as to confuse them.

This approach maintains the primacy of the supernatural in a two-fold way. First, Catholic theology must correctly emphasize the formality and distinctiveness of the supernatural mystery as such, essentially differentiated from the objects of natural knowledge. The point of such an emphasis is to underscore the gratuity or gift-character of divine revelation as a grace, to be sure, and the inaccessibility of the mystery of Christianity to unaided human nature. No amount of unaided human rationalization can justify or give sufficiently warranted foundation to the distinctively inspired supernatural belief in the mysteries of Christianity. However, this emphasis on distinction also allows us to underscore the real capacity of supernatural revelation to act as a transcendent measure on all truth claims of a natural human kind.[58] Due to its superior character,

---

58. Söhngen, "The Analogy of Faith: Unity in the Science of Faith," 193:

The analogy of faith is the analogy of being incorporated into the analogy of faith and standing under its rule. There are four relationships within this analogy of faith ... 1. Epistemologically there is the service of knowing in faith, whereby in and from faith we know more than we did before. 2. Ontologically there is the elevation of nature by grace, nature taken here according to its pure essence. 3. In terms of salvation history, there is the salvation of nature by grace, nature now seen it its historical circumstances. 4. For the order of knowing and

divine revelation can perform this function without supplanting the distinctive work of natural reasoning as such. One can realize by the light of theological reflection on revelation that a given philosophical claim is erroneous or problematic, but the philosophical demonstration that this is the case remains a work of philosophical reasoning as such, stemming from natural premises of reason, and attaining natural conclusions. Divine revelation acts as a critical light shining actively on human reason, then, in which fallible human arguments of the human sciences are subject to critical scrutiny and discernment in comparison with the givens of divine truth. It does so in such a way as to preserve, defend, stimulate, and exalt natural human reason, not supplant or suppress it.

"Christian" philosophy appears in this light as something of a misnomer but not entirely so. Considered according to specification or with respect to the formal object of study, philosophy is not Christian as such, nor are the natural sciences, nor could they ever be, since the human mind has no natural access to the mystery of the Holy Trinity. We know of the Trinity only by grace and the gift of divine revelation and not by the aptitude of our natural human powers of philosophical reasoning, historical investigation, or scientific discovery. Thus the formal objects of the natural disciplines of philosophy, history, and the sciences arise from our reflection on merely natural experience and our limited and fallible rational investigation of the structure, causes, and principles of reality.[59] However, we can speak of a two-fold theological qualification of the activity of this natural intellectual life in its concrete historical exercise. One pertains to the effect of objects of supernatural knowledge upon the consideration of natural objects of knowledge. The other pertains to the effects of grace upon the interior dispositions of the human person who seeks the natural truth.[60]

---

language there is the reestablishment of the obscured Book of Nature in the Book of Scripture.

59. On Christian philosophy, see especially Georges Cottier, *Les chemins de la raison: Questions d'épistémologie théologique et philosophique* (Paris: Parole et Silence, 1997).

60. See arguments to this effect in Thomas Joseph White, *Wisdom in the Face of*

Regarding the effect of supernatural objects, yes, human philosophy, historical study, and scientific learning have their own native objects and domains, perhaps intrinsically open to divine revelation but formally distinct from it. And yet in the concrete historical exercise of the life of the mind, the human person and human historical cultures more generally are affected profoundly by their acceptance or refusal or mere native ignorance of the mystery of God revealed in Christ. Consequently, the objects of divine revelation made manifest in faith (realities like that of the existence of God the Holy Trinity, the mystery of the creation, the reality of the spiritual soul, or the eschatological destiny of the person) alert the human person *qua* philosopher or historian or scientist to the possibility of the study of objects of natural reason as such that align closely with or that are included within those truths formally revealed by supernatural revelation (the so-called *praeambula fidei*). The Christian philosopher, for example, can concern himself *as a philosopher* with topics such as the rationality of belief in God, the natural desire to see God, the philosophical intelligibility of the notion of creation, the demonstration of the existence of the spiritual soul, the metaphysics of human personhood, or various objective moral judgments of human acts.

Second, then, grace affects the interior dispositions of the person who seeks the natural truth in a given domain. A person who is adversely disposed to the truths of the Christian religion (whether in the theoretical or practical intellect, the inclinations of the will, moral habits, or the attachments of the emotions and instincts) will in the concrete exercise of human reasoning be likely to resolve inwardly to study arguments that weigh against Christian belief in one way or another, or will more likely simply resist or remain indifferent to arguments that weigh in its favor.[61] He may also belong to a culture that is largely ignorant of the Christian mystery and that,

---

Modernity: A Study in Thomistic Natural Theology, 2nd ed. (Naples, FL: Sapientia Press, 2016), Appendix C.

61. On the influence of the will upon the intellectual considerations of truth, see Aquinas, *De malo*, q. 6.

due to this fact, is subject a number of existential disadvantages—of ignorance, moral weakness, distrust, or outright hostility. Likewise, the transformative inward effects of grace are such that a person who becomes deeply disposed to the mystery of God revealed in Christ is likely also to experience profound existential alterations of disposition in mind, will, and sensate affectivity. What is true of persons individually is also true for communities, cultures, and societies, which exert various forms of conventional influence over the course of human reasoning generally in any given historical and temporal setting.

The admission of a relative autonomy of specification in the order of natural knowledge brings with it incumbent responsibilities within Catholic theology to forms of progress and discovery that arise within the domain of natural reason. New philosophical, natural scientific, sociological, or historical discoveries, if genuine, belong to the universal patrimony of human rationality and therefore have a place within the larger body of human wisdom that is itself informed by the divine wisdom of revelation. Catholic theology must remain docile from within, as it were, to the ongoing process of natural reason, which aspires to fulfillment not only external to but especially from within the exercise of Catholic reflection on reality.

For Catholic theology, there is a bridge through philosophy to the natural sciences and other disciplines of learning. The mediation of knowledge of natural realities as they relate to supernatural truth is conducted by philosophical metaphysics and philosophy of nature insofar as these latter are intrinsically open (not intrinsically inclined however) to the manifestation of revealed truth. The integration and differentiation of supernatural revelation and natural knowledge is conducted by Catholic theological science insofar as the latter shows itself capable of addressing, assimilating and even making use of philosophical and natural truths within theology as such.

ON THE MUTUAL COMPATIBILITY OF DESCENDING
AND ASCENDANT WISDOM

In conclusion, then, we can speak of the necessity of articulating thematically both a descending and an ascendant wisdom, each of which plays a role in Catholic theology informed by both the *analogia fidei* and the *analogia entis*. Theological wisdom by its very nature depends upon divine revelation and is therefore a descending form of wisdom, originating from above and outside the sphere of human intellectual accomplishment, given gratuitously in its first principles and final purposes. The study of the *analogia fidei*, of the inner intelligibility of the mysteries of Christianity, allows us to explore the internal structure and meaning of the deposit of faith. This study can assimilate into itself and even make constructive use of ineradicably human forms of knowledge—be they philosophical, modern scientific, or historical—and must do so if it wishes to provide a sufficiently realistic and comprehensive vision of the Christological revelation of God, as it is truly given to human beings in the midst of their ordinary experience and natural forms of knowledge.

Philosophical wisdom is "ascendant" in relation to divine revelation only insofar as it is the natural intellectual medium by virtue of which human beings may arrive rationally at posing ultimate questions regarding the origins and purposes of existence, the physical cosmos, living things, and human rational animals in particular. It is this ascendant sphere of inquiry that allows human beings to ask, and even answer in natural forms of reasoning, questions pertaining to the existence of God, the nature of the human person, the dignity of the spiritual soul, and the question of our human destiny in the face of death. The two forms of wisdom are distinct but complementary and potentially interactive. The philosophical form of wisdom can be exercised from within the theological form and in subordination to its higher and more ultimate ends. It is this form of balanced, sapiential reflection that permits traditional Catholic theology to thrive and to transcend the trends and dead-ends of human reflection across differences of time and culture. If cultivated in our contemporary setting it is this form of theology that can provide measured reflection within the Catholic Church, in the face of a host of pressing and legitimate modern and contemporary concerns.

In comparison with the modern rival tendencies of a 'theological anthropology' and a postmodern "Christological ontology," such a form of reflection is marked by several noteworthy differences. While Schleiermacher and Barth each sought to conceptualize theology 'after the Copernican revolution' of Kantianism, modern Catholic theology (following Söhngen) must seek to rethink the philosophical capabilities of the human person in light of divine revelation and the healing effects of the grace of Christ. The ascendant aspirations of the metaphysical knowledge of God come into their full maturity only in light of and in response to the descendant initiative of revelation, as the grace of Christ stimulates and purifies the initiatives of human nature. A theology structured in this way stands in fundamental organic continuity with the metaphysical tradition of the Church, in both its patristic and scholastic modes, while also standing open to modern insights, questions and discoveries, including those of the modern sciences. Philosophy plays a key role in mediating the conversation between the modern sciences and dogmatic theology but should do so in such a way as to help manifest the unity of divine revelation and scientific learning, not their pretended antithesis.

According to this understanding, theology understood as *sacra doctrina* does not have its inward content *determined* per se by philosophical reflection on the *analogia entis*, but it is conditioned by it, since it makes use of the natural range of ontological thinking to understand better the distinctly revealed mysteries of the faith. There is a Catholic 'and' at work in this line of thinking: Trinitarian theology *and* the metaphysics of classical monotheism, the mystery of the hypostatic union *and* the philosophical study of the divine and human essences of Christ, theological anthropology based in an Augustinian understanding of grace *and* Thomistic hylomorphism, divine law *and* virtue theory. At the same time, this same form of thinking can

recognize that in principle a structured form of philosophical ontology can be extracted from theological reflection and understood
according to its own principles based on the natural use of human
reason. Consequently, this holistically theological form of thought is
compatible with a classical (non-postmodern) philosophical realism
that is theocentric in orientation. The First Vatican Council retains
all its normativity for Catholic theology in this regard:

> There is a two-fold order of knowledge, distinct not only in principle but
> also in object; in principle, because in the one we know by natural reason,
> in the other by divine faith; in object because apart from what natural rea-
> son can attain, there are proposed to our belief mysteries that are hidden
> in God that can never be known unless they are revealed by God.... Never-
> theless, if reason illumined by faith inquires in an earnest, pious, and sober
> manner, it attains by God's grace a certain understanding of the mysteries,
> which is most fruitful, *both from the analogy with the objects of its natural
> knowledge* and *from the connection of these mysteries with one another and
> with man's ultimate end.*[62]

Both the *analogia entis* and the *analogia fidei* are key to modern
Catholic theology, and each have a distinct intelligibility, while rest-
ing in profound mutual harmony with one another. Standing upon
these twin foundations of philosophical and theological realism,
Christian theologians may learn to serve God the Holy Trinity with
wisdom, obedience, joy, and love.

62. First Vatican Council, *Dei Filius*, ch. 4, emphasis added. Translation taken from
Heinrich Denzinger, *Compendium of Creeds, Definitions, and Declarations on Matters of
Faith and Morals*, 43rd edition, ed. P. Hünermann, R. Fastiggi, and A. E. Nash (San Fran-
cisco: Ignatius Press, 2012), para. 3015–16. [Hereafter, "*Denzinger*."].

2

On the Nexus of Mysteries
The Center of the Science of Theology

Catholic theology seeks to study and understand the mysteries of Christianity in their inner intelligibility and inner-connection. The New Testament often employs the term "mystery" in the singular, referring, for example, to the "*mysterion*" revealed in Christ. St. Paul describes this mystery as something hidden in God, now made known in Jesus of Nazareth. "To me ... this grace was given, to preach to the Gentiles the unsearchable riches of Christ, and to make all men see what is the plan of the mystery hidden for ages in God who created all things" (Eph. 3:8–9). "To them God chose to make known how great among the Gentiles are the riches of the glory of this mystery, which is Christ in you, the hope of glory" (Col. 1:27). "Great indeed, we confess, is the mystery of our religion: He was manifested in the flesh, vindicated in the Spirit, seen by angels, preached among the nations, believed on in the world, taken up in glory" (1 Tim. 3:16). In these passages, mystery signifies God the Father himself, as he is now made known in Christ, his Son. The Son has made him known by coming into the world to effectuate the filial adoption of human beings by grace, such that through God's election in Christ, they might become children of God. Thus the mystery in this singular sense is inclusive and polyphonic: it concerns God in himself and the plans of God, by which he acts to divinize his creation eschatologically. The Incarnation and the resurrection of Christ make known this beginning and end of all things: the mystery of God in himself as it is communicated to his creation.[1]

In a complementary and noncompetitive sense then, we can speak of the mystery in question in a plural signification: there are mysteries of Christianity. These are truths originally inaccessible to mere unaided natural reason, supernatural truths, made known by way of revelation and by the grace of faith. Such supernatural truths include the Trinitarian identity of God himself, but also the unfolding of the divine economy: creation, the mystery of human beings as made in the image of God, the original sin and its consequences, God's covenant with Israel, the mystery of Christ, the Incarnate Son, the life of the Virgin Mary, the sacraments in their organic unity, and the Church as the mystical body of Christ. Such examples can be multiplied or illustrated in increasing degrees of detail. In any of these cases, the mysteries of Christianity are not only gratuitously revealed by God, but are also super-intelligible, not in the sense of being incomprehensible, but in the sense of being richer in intrinsic intelligibility than one can understand comprehensively. Although not initially intelligible to unaided reason, they are, with God's grace, both luminous and obscure, open to continual understanding and further pondering.

They are also united or related to one another. The various mysteries of the Catholic faith stem from one divine wisdom or logic and manifest and indicate obliquely that wisdom. In this sense, they are not only mysteries related to one another (as the Incarnation is related to the Eucharist, and vice versa), but they are also in a sense all contained within and united as the one "mystery" revealed in Christ, that singular mystery mentioned above, indicated by St. Paul: God made known in his economy.

---

1. See on this topic Louis Bouyer, *Mysterion: Du mystère à la mystique* (Paris: Cerf, 2017).

How in Catholic theology does one come to understand each singular mystery? How do the mysteries relate to one another, especially by analogical resemblance? How or in what sense are they related hierarchically, so that there is a hierarchy of mysteries? I would like to explore these three questions briefly below, with pertinent historical and doctrinal examples. The aim is only to gesture to the fullness of a Catholic theological account, in a succinct way, while also indicating clearly some general norms of thought that are at the center of the nature of Catholic theology. I will study, then, the apophatic and kataphatic dimensions of mystery, the analogical resemblances between them, and their causal configurations, which allow us to understand them in their hierarchy and order. Having indicated these dimensions of the study of mystery in Catholic theology, we can understand better the inward unity of Catholic reflection on revelation and the central role that a specifically theological application of analogical thinking plays within it.

THE ESSENCE OF A MYSTERY: SUPERNATURAL OBSCURITY AND INNER INTELLIGIBILITY

How do theologians seek to understand and identify in conceptual and verbal terms the essence or core of a mystery? Here we may consider a series of speculative practices that are typical in the process of identification of essential mystery and illustrate them briefly by historical examples.

The Primacy of the Apophatic: Negations of Extreme Errors, Often Opposed Logically to One Another, Lead Us toward The Intelligible Inner Ground of Mystery

A first speculative rule of reasoning in theological consideration of mystery concerns the negation of conceptions of the mystery that are to be excluded. Historically speaking this frequently occurs through the identification of extreme errors of theology, opposed to one another in some respect, such that the rejection of either of two opposed and erroneous positions (each considered in error under a different aspect) leads the gaze of the mind back toward the just center between the two extremes. Illustrations help to clarify this important idea. Consider briefly some examples from theological controversy and dogmatic clarifications.

The Mystery of the Trinity

Early disputes regarding the New Testament depiction of God, entailing the question of the personal distinction of the Father, Son and Spirit, and the question of their unity, led to diverse problematic positions, at times clearly opposed by extremes. The third century Sabellian or modalist error, for example, consisted in the affirmation of the divinity of the Son and Spirit but denial of their personal distinctness in God, while the Arian heresy consisted in the affirmation of the real distinction of the persons but the denial of their unity or equality of nature, as the one God.[2] The two positions are opposed on both the distinction of persons and the unity of essence. One position is correct in underscoring the divinity of the Son and Spirit and in error in denying the real distinction of persons, while the other is correct in affirming the distinction of persons and in error regarding the affirmation of the Son and the Spirit as mere creatures, since the Son and the Spirit are one in being and essence (*homoousios*) with the Father. The opposed positions, then, are each deficient in a key respect, since neither can conceive of personal distinction while also affirming unity of essence. The truth of the faith, and the core of the mystery of the Trinity, comes into focus once one must begin to think constructively about the real distinction of the three persons who are one in essence and being. The inscape or inner intelligibility of the mystery begins to appear in light of the notion of eternal processions of distinct persons in God, who are

2. See on this point Khaled Anatolios, *Retrieving Nicaea: The Development and Meaning of Trinitarian Doctrine* (Grand Rapids, MI: Baker Academic, 2011), 22–23, 42–98; Thomas Joseph White, *The Trinity: On the Nature and Mystery of the One God* (Washington, DC: The Catholic University of America Press, 2022), chapter 7; Aquinas provides a helpful analysis of the logical contraries of Sabellianism and Arianism in *ST* I, q. 27, a. 1.

consubstantial, a notion that has greater clarity once we have confronted these two opposed extremes.

Christology

A similar example is provided from the consideration of the Nestorian and monophysite positions in 5th century Christology.[3] Nestorius seems in practice to have referred to Jesus of Nazareth as a man having a hypostatic singularity or individuality distinct from that of the person of the Son of God, who united himself to the singular individual, Jesus, in the Incarnation. He affirmed two distinct natures in Christ but also two distinct subjects or personal individual loci, that of the person of the Son and that of the man Jesus. Monophysite theology by contrast affirmed one hypostatic subject of the Word made flesh but denied the real distinction of two natures after the union. The two positions disagree and are opposed on both the question of the number of personal subjects and the number of natures. Chalcedonian orthodoxy, which emerged from a consideration of these opposed positions, rightly underscored the real distinction of the two natures (divine and human) united in the one hypostasis (and person) of the Word made flesh. The mystery is found then in the personal subsistence of the Word not only in a divine nature but also in a human nature.

The Eucharist

Controversies over the Eucharistic mystery in the 9th century led to the emergence of twin positions, mutually opposed to one another. Paschasius Radbertus affirmed that the true body of Christ is rendered present in the Eucharist and so the very properties of the glorified body and blood of Christ are in some way affected by consumption. Ratramnus responded by arguing that the heavenly body of Christ in its properties is not affected by consumption of the Eucharist and so it is not reasonable to speak of the true presence of

---

3. See on this topic, Brian Daley, *God Visible: Patristic Christology Reconsidered* (Oxford: Oxford University Press, 2018), 10–15, 174–99.

the heavenly Christ rendered present in the consecration of the Eucharist.[4] The genuine articulation of the mystery is located in the affirmation of the true presence of the body and blood of Christ in the Eucharist, such as affirmed by Radbertus, while holding that the consumption of the properties of the Eucharist does not alter the physical properties of the glorified Christ, as Ratramnus accurately affirmed.

Grace

Although it is not a matter of doctrinal definition in the same way as the first three examples considered above, the topic of grace may be subject to a similar treatment from diverse and complementary angles. If one is to ask the question what grace is and how it may be identified conceptually, two extremes that are erroneous and opposed to one another arise in historical disputations. One extreme consists in the idea that there is no created grace, and that grace is something wholly divine (God himself) or at least an activity and effect of God that always remains extrinsic to the human person.[5] A contrary position affirms that grace is intrinsic to the person, thus created, but essentially identical with the very substance and nature

4. On these controversies, see Owen M. Phelan, "Horizontal and Vertical Theologies: 'Sacraments' in the Works of Paschasius Radbertus and Ratramnus of Corbie," *The Harvard Theological Review* 103, no. 3 (July 2010): 271–89, and the encyclopedic consideration of twelfth and thirteenth century theological reception and interpretation controversies regarding the Eucharist, Jörgen Vijgen, *The Status of Eucharistic Accidents "sine subiecto": An Historical Survey up to Thomas Aquinas and Selected Reactions* (Berlin: Walter de Gruyter, 2013).

5. Eastern Orthodox Christians sometimes claim that the western scholastic notion of created grace is theologically problematic and that instead one must speak uniquely of the uncreated energies of God as the referent when one speaks of grace. Interestingly, John Meyendorff has pointed out that Gregory of Palamas is not opposed per se to the use of the notion of created grace when speaking of the effects of deification in the human person. See his *A Study of Gregory Palamas*, trans. G. Lawrence (Crestwood, NY: St. Vladimir's Seminary Press, 1974), 164. Aquinas for his part argues that grace is an effect of God created in the human person so as to elevate the person supernaturally to the enjoyment of God in himself, who is uncreated. In other words, the creation of grace is from God and for God, allowing the creature to participate in the uncreated life of God. It is the ontological condition of divinization, not its created substitute, as is sometimes mistakenly thought. See *ST* I-II, q. 110, a. 1.

of man (so that grace is substantial as it were, and all that one is as a person results from grace).[6] The genuine and mysterious position that stands between the two is one that affirms that grace is created in the human person as a (mere) property of the person, albeit one that is truly inwardly transformative and of essential soteriological importance. Here again, however, we arrive at two potential errors opposed by extremes. One may speak of grace erroneously either as identical with the activity of one faculty (that is to say, as identical with the act of faith in the intellect or charity in the will), or as identical with the whole soul, as such, in a quasi-substantial way. The first perspective is overly reductive as it locates grace in one activity alone, such as in charity. The latter is too extensive, as it depicts grace to be something quasi-identical with the spiritual soul as such in all that it is and does. The position between these two opposed errors is that which sees grace as a quality of the soul that is sufficiently "profound" as to its ontological location in the soul—or radical in root—so as to affect all faculties of the soul and their exercise, especially the twin spiritual faculties of intellect and will, which are qualified inwardly especially (so Aquinas argues) by the exercise of faith, hope, charity, and the infused moral virtues, as well as the gifts of the Holy Spirit.[7] This position is opposed to both a mere grace extrinsicism, which posits no inward transformation of the human nature of the person, and a grace integralism, which posits no original distinction in personal beings between personal nature and personal grace.

6. This seems to have been the position of Michael Baius and is among the positions condemned by Pope Pius V in his papal bull of 1567 *Ex omnibus afflictionibus*. This can be found in Heinrich Denzinger, *Compendium of Creeds, Definitions, and Declarations on Matters of Faith and Morals*, 43rd edition, ed. P. Hünermann, R. Fastiggi and A. E. Nash (San Francisco: Ignatius Press, 2012), §§1901–80, esp. 1–7. [Hereafter, "*Denzinger.*"]

7. Aquinas posits that grace is something "deeper" than a virtue, but it is exhibited in the virtues, as we will return to below. (See on this point, *ST* I-II, q. 110.) However, he also posits that the natural virtues that pertain to the moral life (prudence, justice, fortitude, temperance) must be transformed and elevated from within by infused moral virtue, so as to be oriented to the new and higher end presented by grace, and so that they may be assimilated to the infused theological virtues of faith, hope, and love, and also so disposed by grace to the imprint and activity of the gifts of the Holy Spirit. On infused moral virtues, see *ST* I-II, q. 63, a. 2 and q. 65, aa. 2–3.

The Development of Doctrine

The very characterization of extremes with regard to the theological notion of the development of doctrine is controverted in nature, notwithstanding the fact that there is some affirmation of such development as organic progress in the Second Vatican Council Constitution on Divine Revelation, *Dei Verbum*.[8] One extreme consists simply in the denial of this idea, by the claim that there is no organic unfolding of teachings and practices in the Church over time (since they are unchanging and historically non-developmental). The other extreme consists in the erroneous claim that the life of the Church and the propositional logic of her teaching can be contradictory or opposed to themselves over time.[9] On this view there is not organic development in what John Henry Newman characterized as occuring in logically consistent ways, but rather there is a change across time that entails real intellectual ruptures and substantial oppositions of position. The truth of the mystery indicated between these two extremes, as it were, is concerned with the notes or properties of ongoing life and teaching in the Church as it develops in continuity. There are diverse doctrinal teachings across time (such as those concerning the possibility of salvation outside the visible Church, or the rights of religious freedom) or diverse applications of principles of the moral life in changing historical circumstances (concerning slavery, usury, the death penalty, and in other domains) that may seem initially to contradict one another either in logical form or in concrete practice. However, the study of the mystery of the developmental life and teaching of the Church invites one to identify a deeper consistency of principle and a nuanced application of enduring or similar principles in new contexts and historical conditions. From

8. See Dogmatic Constitution on Divine Revelation, *Dei Verbum* in *Vatican Council II*, vol. 1: *The Conciliar and Post Conciliar Documents*, ed. A. Flannery (Northport, NY: Costello Publ. Co., 2004), §8.

9. Alfred Loisy, *Prelude to the Modernist Crisis: The "Firmin" Articles of Alfred Loisy*, trans. Christine Thirlway, ed. C. J. T. Talar (Oxford: Oxford University Press, 2010); and the study of Aidan Nichols, *From Newman to Congar: The Idea of Development from the Victorians to the Second Vatican Council* (Edinburgh: T&T Clark, 1990).

this latter form of thinking there emerges a portrait of the Church's life and its doctrinal development across time that is characterized by internal consistency, progressively emergent clarity, and living vigor.

Kataphatic Indications: Identifying the Conceptual Location and Inscape of Mysteries

From the exclusions of contrary extremes one may focus in on the intelligible content of mysteries as such, not merely by way of exclusion of errors opposed to the inward sense of the faith but also by way of an assessment and positive assertion of the inward essence of mysteries. The theologian does not just seek to say what mysteries are not, but also what they consist in. Toward this end, several key components of positive study of mysteries must be kept in mind.

First, the assessment of the inward form of a mystery maintains the primacy of the judgment of supernatural faith and its ecclesial context over and above or prior to the theological concepts of particular schools of thought or the constructions of various individual theologians. That is to say, the Church and her members enjoy by a certain instinct of supernatural faith a connatural familiarity with the mysteries of the faith, such as those mentioned above: the inner life of God as Trinity, the mystery of Christ as the Word incarnate, the Eucharistic real presence of God, the indwelling mystery of grace, and the developmental life of the Church. By the act of faith, the human mind attains directly to "the first truth," as Aquinas notes, notably the mystery of the Holy Trinity (God in himself), and the supernatural knowledge that judges all things in light of the Trinity. This ecclesial and personal judgment expresses itself always in some linguistic and conceptual form, even from the beginning of the New Testament and the early formulas of the Church, as expressed in the Creed, the councils, basic doctrinal formulations, the teachings of doctors, the traditions of theological schools, and so forth. Moreover the judgment of faith always has need of conceptual and linguistic formulations, but the latter are that in which the judgment of the Church transpires, not that in which the judgment terminates. The supernatural judgment of the Church and her membership terminates in the reality itself, of supernatural mystery. It follows that, because the mystery itself is only ever understood imperfectly and non-comprehensively, further conceptual precision, exploration, and enrichment of reflection is possible. Conceptual formulations can be truly "adequate" to the mysteries of the faith, so as to indicate in truth what God is or the character of the mysteries, but such formulations are never exhaustive. Schools of theology that seek enriched and more subtle conceptual explorations of the Church's confession of faith are inevitable and even necessary and salutary, as they contribute to the zealous and loving exploration of the inward content of mystery, but they are also always relative to the Church in her life and collective judgment of the mysteries of the faith, which is given prior and posterior to any constructions of the schools and as encompassing the latter, as various movements of life within herself.

Second, all positive doctrinal and theological formulations regarding the inward form of mystery make use of a philosophical metaphysics of some kind but also make use of such notions "analogically" to signify and speak realistically about something that is not properly intelligible only from within the range of natural understanding. For example, one may speak of the conversion of bread and wine into the body and blood of Christ, in the Eucharist, in terms of "transubstantiation," but in doing so one is not merely speaking of the metaphysics of substances as one does with respect to the ordinary objects of natural knowledge. In speaking in this theological register one denotes a mystery in the proper sense, something accessible only to human reason given the grace of faith and the understanding it provides, while one also simultaneously denotes the ontological dimension of this mystery by an analogy that is properly speaking theological, one that is distinct from the analogical attributions of metaphysics.[10] The theological usage of concepts drawn

10. See on this point the suggestive reflections by Jacques Maritain, *Approches sans Entraves*, ch. 12, sections 1–4, in *Oeuvres Complète* vol. XIII (Fribourg and Paris: Éditions Universitaires and Éditions Saint-Paul, 1992).

from philosophy retains something of the natural metaphysical significations of these concepts even while transposing them into domains where there are registers of signification that mere philosophical uses of the terms in question do not entail. The change of bread and wine into the body and blood of Christ truly is substantial (pertaining to the whole individual being and the unified nature of a thing), but the substantial change in kind is mysteriously different from that of any merely natural change and is numinous in kind. The relations of Trinitarian persons are truly relations, in some way like created relations, but they are also wholly other since they are relations that are "subsistent."[11] Examples of this kind of metaphysical use of language transposed into the domain of the formally mysterious as such could be multiplied, and I will return to a variety of examples shortly below.

Third and finally, theological modes of analysis and description of mysteries entail a mixture of kataphatic disclosure (discourse truly adequate to "what" the mystery is essentially, that denotes it really to the mind in faith) and apophatic discourse, which recognizes the incomprehensibility of the mystery and the limits of theological understanding. One way to restate this is to note that the first element named above (the negative exclusion of erroneous extremes or errant conceptual claims) remains even alongside and "within" the positive discourse that seeks to disclose truly and accurately what the mystery in question is. Likewise, there is the apophaticism of that which has just been mentioned: the mysteries in question transcend all our natural concepts and their typical range of significations, even analogical ones, and so even when carefully re-purposed in the context of theological practice for specifically supernatural use, such concepts can signify the mysteries of God only imperfectly. The obscurity of the mystery as transcending our natural comprehension remains, as does the imperfection of our mode of knowledge, which occurs by means of faith, in the judgment of faith, rather than by immediate perception.

11. See, for example, Aquinas, *ST* I, q. 29, a. 4.

It follows from what has been said that there are possibly better and worse descriptions of mysteries, presented by diverse theologians, and diverse schools of theology, based on a variety of factors, namely, (1) the problematic theories and ideas of the mysteries they mean rightly and accurately to exclude, (2) the positive conceptual notions they develop to indicate the mystery in its proper intelligibly and mystery, (3) the use of metaphysical concepts or the "philosophical instruments" of the work in question, and (4) the right awareness of the kataphatic and apophatic contours of what is known luminously and what remains obscure in the Church's apprehension of the mystery in its proper essence or inscape.

In light of these various qualifying remarks, we can now return to our five examples from the first part of this chapter to give positive examples of concepts (some of which I am taking from the Thomistic school) elaborated "supra-analogically" so as to denote the mysteries of the faith in themselves. These ideas help illustrate something of the notion of the designation of the essence of mystery that we have mentioned above.

The Mystery of the Trinity: Denoting Trinitarian Persons as "Subsistent Relations"

We noted above that the classical Trinitarian controversies in the early Church led to the negation of two extremes: the position that affirmed the divinity of Father, Son, and Spirit but denied the real distinction of persons in God and the position that affirmed the real distinction of the persons but denied the divinity and consubstantiality of the Son and the Spirit with the Father. The truth "between" these two extremes is found in the twin affirmations of the real distinction of the persons and the true and plenary deity of the three persons, who are each the one God. The Son is God from God, light from light, true God from true God, and the same can be said as well of the Holy Spirit.

The early Church, in figures like Gregory of Nazianzus and Augustine, discerned that the way to move forward in the theological consideration of the mystery of the Trinity was to consider the distinction of the persons in God in terms of eternal relations of origin.[12] These relations arise from the eternal processions, of the Son and the Spirit from the Father, so that one understands the Son originating from all eternity from the Father by generation and the Spirit by way of spiration. In these two processions the persons of the Son and the Spirit receive from the Father all that he is as God (the plenitude of the divine nature). The Spirit likewise (in Augustine's thought) is the eternal love, who proceeds relationally from the Father and the Son as their mutual gift and bond of charity.[13]

It was Augustine already in *The Trinity* who saw that the relations in God could not be merely properties or "accidents" of the divine "substance," since the persons are in a sense defined by their relationality.[14] It is that which distinguishes them from one another, since they are "otherwise" each truly God in all that they are. If the three persons are each the one God, and if they are truly distinguished principally by their relations of origin, then the relations "define" what they are as persons. In the thirteenth century the scholastic doctors, especially Bonaventure and Thomas Aquinas, formulated the notion of "subsistent relations" to give articulation in a more precise and illuminating way to this idea of the numinous distinction of persons of God.[15] Here one can think of a two-fold way of thinking of each person, as (1) relationally distinct from the others and (2) as true God (having the plenitude of the divine nature common to

12. See, for example, Gregory of Nazianzus, *Oration 29*, no. 16 and Augustine, *The Trinity*, 5.1.6. [Gregory of Nazianzus, *On God and Christ: The Five Theological Orations and Two Letters to Cledonius*, trans. F. Williams and L. Wickham (Crestwood, NY: St. Vladimir's Seminary Press, 2002); Augustine, *The Trinity*, ed. J. E. Rotelle, trans. E. Hill (Hyde Park, NY: New City Press, 1991).]

13. Augustine, *The Trinity*, 4.5.29; 5.3.12–15; 15.5.37.

14. Augustine, *The Trinity*, 5.1.6. See the analysis of Lewis Ayres, *Augustine and the Trinity* (Cambridge: Cambridge University Press, 2010), 268–72.

15. See, for example, Aquinas, *ST* I, q. 29, a. 4, and Bonaventure, *Comm. I Sent.*, d. 33, a. un, q. 1 [*Commentaria in quatuor libros Sententiarum*, 4 vols. (Quaracchi: Ex Typographia Collegii S. Bonaventurae, 1882–89)]. See also the commentary of Russell Friedman, *Medieval Trinitarian Thought from Aquinas to Ockham* (Cambridge: Cambridge University Press, 2013), 11–13, 32–41, 109–13, 171–73.

each person).[16] So the Father is the relational origin of all that is (for Aquinas, he "is" his paternity in all that he is[17]), and the Father is truly God, having all that pertains to the numinous life and essence of the divine within himself. The Son is the eternally begotten Logos or Word (understood by similitude to the intellectual procession in human thought of the concept from the thinking subject), who is filial or begotten in all that he is, and the Son is truly God, having in himself from the Father the plenitude of perfection proper to the mysterious and transcendent life and essence of God.[18] The Spirit is the eternally spirated Love of the Father and the Son, their mutual uncreated love and gift, whom they spirate as from one principle, and he contains in himself all that they are as God, the plenitude of the divine life and essence.[19] The notion of subsistent relations, then, is quite rich when it is explored in its depths and implications. It leads one into the notion of each of the three persons as related in all that he is to the others and as each truly and fully God in all that he is, so that each person is truly distinct and each person is truly God. The affirmations we found ourselves with at the start, in the rejection of opposed errors, are brought together in a deepened appreciation of the inward contours of the ultimate mystery of Christianity, the mystery of the unity and distinction of the Trinitarian persons. The "relations" in God are analogous, like and unlike those of personal creatures, as are the divine "persons," who are not human persons, and the "divine nature" which is wholly other than and transcendent of creaturely nature. However, the theologically formulated terms of figures like Bonaventure and Aquinas, following Augustine, do allow us to gain imperfect insight and understand non-comprehensively the inward mystery of God.

---

16. See the analysis of Gilles Emery in "Essentialism or Personalism in the Treatise on God in St. Thomas Aquinas?," *The Thomist* 64, no. 4 (2000): 521–63.

17. See Aquinas, *ST* I, q. 33, a. 2; q. 40, a. 1.

18. Aquinas, *ST* I, q. 34, aa. 1–2.

19. Aquinas, *ST* I, qq. 36–37.

Christology: Hypostatic Subsistence in Two Natures

We noted above that the Chalcedonian Christological definition rejected the twin errors of those positions that deny or obscure the unity of the person of Christ (due to his two natures) or that deny or obscure the real distinction of the two natures (due to his unity of person). The positive truth that stands between these two extremes is found in the notion of Christ as one divine person subsisting in two natures, perfectly divine and perfectly human, where the natures are truly distinct but not separate, and where the actions of each are integral (dyothelitism) and coordinated in symphony and hierarchy so that the human nature of the Lord is subordinate to and is the instrument of his divine person and his divine life.[20]

To speak of this mystery, theologians have coined the term "hypostatic union," a notion originating from Cyril of Alexandria.[21] As Aquinas notes, the union in question is one of the two natures "within" the one divine hypostasis, that is to say, within the personal subject of the Son.[22] Aquinas notes that the hypostatic union of the divine and human natures within the one person of the Son is a "substantial union," meaning that the divine and human natures in Christ are not united in the way two distinct substances or realities are united accidentally or by a mere property of relationality.[23] Two human beings united by a moral cooperation in a joint activity enjoy

20. See, for example, the Third Council of Constantinople [*Denzinger*, §§550–59]; John Damascene, *An Exposition of the Orthodox Faith*, III, c. 15, in *Nicene and Post-Nicene Fathers*, second series, vol. 9, ed. P. Schaff and H. Wace, trans. E. W. Watson and L. Pullan (Buffalo, NY: Christian Literature Publishing, 1899); and Aquinas, *ST* III, q. 19.

21. See Cyril of Alexandria, Second Letter to Nestorius:

We do not say that the Logos became flesh by having his nature changed, nor for that matter that he was transformed into a complete human being composed out of soul and body. On the contrary, we say that in an unspeakable and incomprehensible way, the Logos united to himself, in his hypostasis, flesh enlivened by a rational soul, and in this way became a human being and has been designated "Son of Man." In *The Christological Controversy*, ed. and trans. R. A. Norris, Jr. (Philadelphia: Fortress Press, 1980), 132–33.

22. Aquinas, *ST* III, q. 2, a. 2.

23. Aquinas, *ST* III, q. 2, a. 6.

a relational union of a habitual kind, since they work together regularly, but they are not truly one in being or united in a singular person or singular substance. The man Jesus, however, does not enjoy merely this kind of moral and habitual union of relationality with the eternal Logos.[24] The man Jesus *is* the Logos who has become human. The person in question is one and divine. So the humanity of Jesus is the humanity of God the Son, and the unity of the humanity with the divinity of the Son is a unity *in* the one person. This "substantial union" is only analogous to the substantial unity of a human being, who is one in substance, as a living rational animal, substantially united in body and soul. The reason for the dissimiltude is two-fold: first, any other singular subsistent human being is only one in nature (human nature), and second, any such being has a merely created personhood. The eternal Son of God made man, by contrast, is twofold in nature (truly God and truly man), and he has an uncreated, divine personhood alone (that of the Word). The person of the Incarnate Son, however, while truly God and man, is also only one in subject, similar to a human person created by God in that the human person is one in subject. There is in Christ one personal subject subsisting in two distinct natures, and thus there is truly something we can call in qualified fashion "a substantial union of God and man" that is found only in him. This is what we refer to when we speak of the eternal Son's hypostatic subsistence in two natures.

The Eucharist: Transubstantiation

The Eucharist, as we noted, is a mystery of the ontological conversion of bread and wine into the body and blood of Christ. The classical controversies that ensued over this mystery pitted those who claimed it was the true body, and therefore there is an effect of our actions upon the body, against those who claimed that our actions do not affect the body of Christ in glory but that therefore there is no warrant to claim it is his true body. The Church eventually the

24. See my criticisms of this "Nestorian" notion of accidental union in *The Incarnate Lord*, ch. 1, following Aquinas's criticisms in *ST* III, q. 2, aa. 6, 8, 10, and 11.

appropriated language of "transubstantiation" in the 13th century (at the Fourth Lateran Council[25]) to speak of the mystery, and it was through the ministrations of the Scholastics (especially Aquinas) that one came to distinguish the conversion of substance (from bread and wine to the body and blood of Christ) from the preservation of properties (or "accidents") of bread and wine that remain in the Eucharist as symbols of the mystery contained therein.[26] Aquinas notes that the change of Eucharistic substantial conversion is analogous to natural change through generation and corruption, on the one hand, and analogous to creation, on the other.[27] In substantial natural change of generation and corruption (such as when fire entirely consumes wood) there is a change of one substance into another (as one thing becomes another), and the change is progressive not instantaneous. In creation (such as when God creates a human spiritual soul *ex nihilo*) there is no change of one thing into another, and the creation of the new thing is instantaneous. In Eucharistic conversion, there is the change of one thing into another (as in natural substantial change), but the change is instantaneous and total (as in creation), not gradual, and it pertains at once to the whole substance of bread and to the whole substance of wine, which become, respectively, the true body of Christ and the true blood of Christ. In this unique event, which contains no pure likeness either to the order of natural change or to the order of immediate creation, there is something that remains from the prior reality (the accidental properties of bread and wine), even as the real substance of the glorified body and blood of Christ are rendered truly present. The glorified body and blood are not rendered present primarily through accidents, as when a human person is rendered present in a new place by becoming physically present quantitatively. Instead the very substance of the glorified body and blood are rendered present (the ontological act of being of the glorified Christ in

25. See on this point, *Denzinger*, §802.
26. See the analysis of Aquinas in *ST* III, q. 75, as well as the comprehensive study of the theology in this period on this topic by Vijgen, *Status of Eucharistic Accidents*.
27. Aquinas, *ST* III, q. 75, a. 4.

his body and blood) and for that reason, the accidental properties of the glorified Christ are rendered present *secundum quid*, by accompaniment or concomitance, insofar as the substance of his body and blood are rendered present under the signs of bread and wine.[28] These signs (the accidents of bread and wine that remain truly present) function as symbolic indicators or significations of the mystery contained therein, indicating nourishment, sacrifice, and ecclesial communion.[29] Aquinas's theological analysis does not "explain" the mystery, as if it could be translated or reduced into a merely rational and natural horizon of explanation. Rather it makes use of a comparison with natural changes (of natural conversion or creation) to indicate "where" the mystery of transubstantiation is by analogy with other forms of change, so as to unveil something of the inward divine "logic" of the mystery of transubstantiation as God has in fact structured it through the institutional activity of Christ.

Grace: Quality of the Soul and Entitative Habitus

We noted above that grace can be seen by extremes as either something wholly extrinsic to the human person, so that participation in the life of God by a spiritual creature is taken to be only a direct participation in the divinity itself, without an elevating principle infused intrinsically into the spiritual creature to proportion it from within to divine life, or that grace can be confused with nature, so that the human being is understood to be "originally constituted" by nature in a state of divinization or in view of a life of divinization by its essence and natural end. In the latter case the very "substance" or essence of the human being is always already divinizing or ordered by nature unto the life of God. Classically the Catholic Church has rejected both views: that which is radically extrinsicist, by separating the orders of nature and grace, and that which is integralist, which collapses the real distinction of the orders of nature and grace.

---

28. Aquinas, *ST* III, q. 76, a. 1.
29. Aquinas, *ST* III, q. 79, a. 1.

Aquinas asks rightly if grace pertains to the substance of the human person or to a property, and he notes rightly that the gift of divinizing grace cannot pertain to the substance of the human being but must be a property.[30] If the former were the case, the presence or absence of grace (its "substantial" gain or loss, absence or presence) would result in a new human essence and substance, so that in becoming a Christian one would change species (ceasing to be human altogether to become Christian or becoming human unequivocally for the first time in becoming Christian), and one would be a new individual being (not metaphorically speaking but literally speaking). Meanwhile, non-Christians would not be human persons (or would be the only humans in differentiation from Christians), and they would have to change their individual identities and cease to exist as individuals in order to become Christians. But these are absurd and erroneous views.

If grace is a property of a substance, it cannot be a quantity or a relation, since it is not a corporeal feature as such and cannot be merely extrinsic to human beings, and so it must in fact be a quality of the human person. The human person is newly qualified by being in a state of grace. Furthermore, grace must be a quality that is primarily spiritual in kind, not corporeal, since it pertains principally to the human spiritual soul of the person who is in a state of grace. Grace first and foremost changes the mind and heart of the human person as it transforms from within the inclinations and acts of the inner spiritual life.

What, however, does this inward quality of the person entail? Aquinas asks whether the state of grace is essentially reducible to something akin to a virtue, such as that afforded by faith, hope, or charity.[31] After all these are virtues that newly qualify the activities of the intellect and will in a person who is Christian. Grace cannot be reduced, however, to the life of the infused theological virtues as such, whether faith, hope, or charity, because these presuppose

30. Aquinas, *ST* I-II, q. 110, a. 2.
31. Aquinas, *ST* I-II, q. 110, a. 3.

something more radical at work in the human person, namely, the primal inclination of the human soul toward union with the mystery of the Trinity, which can only emerge within the spiritual faculties of intellect and will if God first acts within the human soul to elevate its natural inclinations "above" the range of their natural horizon and capacity. The human being cannot first naturally incline itself toward the formally supernatural as such (union with God in himself as Trinity) and then wait for God to add the help of infused virtue, but rather God must grant *both* the (ontologically and logically) prior inclination to supernatural life *and* the infused habitual power of cooperation with grace, in faith, hope, and love, if the person is to move him or herself effectively toward God.[32] So grace is something "deeper" than the life of infused virtue that precedes the latter and that expresses itself in the latter.

Furthermore grace cannot be something merely in one spiritual faculty (the intellect *or* the will), since it is present in both by its expression of coordinated life of truth and love, of faith, hope, and charity, which deeply qualify and reorient both faculties toward union with the Trinity.

Consequently, grace is something "in the essence of the soul," more radically present than it would be if it were in only one spiritual faculty, and is something that orients the whole person in his or her state of being and in the personal exercise of knowing and loving, toward God, in all that the person is and does.[33] This radical presence of grace in the essence of the soul is mysteriously not substantial (pertaining to a change in the human essence as such), but it is so radical as to incline the whole person toward a new life in God (supernatural life) so that the person can truly participate in the divine nature. This movement into God affects the whole state of being of the human person, even if it does so "only" by way of a radical property, not by way of substantial change in the strict sense.

Thomists after Aquinas have employed the technical notion of

32. Aquinas, *ST* I-II, q. 62, aa. 1–3.
33. Aquinas, *ST* I II, q. 110, a. 4.

an "entitative habitus" in order to formulate more clearly this distinct theological idea of the mystery of grace. Here the term "entitative" is used to denote not that grace is a substance but that it qualifies the whole of the human substance (the whole person). The term "habitus" is used to indicate a state of being or a stable way of being, as an effect of grace, that affects the whole person. An analogy can be drawn to the state of health in the physical order. If a person is habitually healthy, he enjoys the stable *quality* of health as something that affects his whole person, the very physical substance of his bodily condition. This is something more radical than the health of only one organ or system, such as that of the heart or the circulatory system. Comprehensive health entails the whole being of the person, since the health in question is a property and quality of the whole being. Such qualities are very radical, even if not substantial, as indeed a person can lose his health without ceasing to exist, but the presence of comprehensive health is of significant effect upon the whole of the person. So likewise, the state of grace is one in which the whole person (through the essence of the soul and its powers and their exercise) is affected by spiritual good health and enjoys a habitual state of being in living friendship with God and in perpetual orientation toward perfect union with God in beatitude. The mystery of grace is thus enunciated in these terms not so as to dissolve one's appreciation of the mystery of grace but so as to elevate one's regard to a consideration of the mysterious depths and contours of the mystery, as a living reality we first and foremost experience and live with and secondarily reflect upon by analogy, so as to consider its numinous and supernatural intelligibility as best as we can.

The Development of Doctrine: Organic Ecclesial Life Gradually Traced by a Nuanced and Coherent Propositional Logic

We noted above that the affirmation of a development of doctrine in the life of the Catholic Church is affirmed against the two extremes of those who deny any such development and those who claim that such development entails a life of occasional contradiction, one that

enters into and so disrupts either the very principles or the very logic of the Church's teaching across time. Against these two extremes
one must posit a developmental life in the Church that entails (as
a part of that life) a practice of intellectual clarification (doctrinal expression) that is adequate to the mystery of God, so that the
Church speaks progressively in conceptually clearer and more enriched ways of the inner truth of the primal revelation. In doing so,
the Church speaks in an organically consistent and coherent way
across time, even if the articulations that take place may not always
be readily anticipated or evidently suggested by the temporally and
logically antecedent clarifications of doctrine or symbolic and liturgical practices of the Church. In this case the mystery that is indicated positively is the following. The life of the Church develops in
new circumstances through history, always in a way that is ontologically consistent with itself. This consistency of life in the Church is
not the life of God the Trinity as such, of course, but its consistency and perdurance as well as its continuity of doctrinal teaching is
a created supernatural reflection of the mystery of the Trinity and
the mystery of God, which is alive in the Church by grace. This progressive ecclesial development-of-life-in-consistency can and does
express itself through diverse vital activities of the Church, and
these include (but are not merely reducible to) doctrinal activities.
In short, the Church continually teaches the truth about God and
all things understood in the light of God in a coherent way down
through time.

In the natural realm, biological living beings act in view of five
ends: nutrition, organic growth, self-defense, self-repair, reproduc-
tion. The analogies to spiritual life are present in the development of
the Church's nourishment from the Word of God, sacred Tradition,
and the sacraments (nutrition), doctrinal consideration of the truth
(growth), her doctrinal activities of self-definition (self-defense), her
movements of reform (self-repair and vital development), and the
spiritual fecundity of charity (spiritual fruitfulness). In a wide range
of contingent historical circumstances these processes of a unified

life can take on a wide range of expressions (much like a biological individual or species can develop in a wide array of ways in diverse environmental conditions, through time). However, the mystery is that there is only one Church in and through all the conditions and circumstances of history, and her doctrinal self-expression and self-communication remains one through all time and through all conditions. It is this mystery of organic continuity amidst change that the Church seeks to denote when she speaks of the mystery of the development of doctrine, as an integral dimension of the ongoing life and vital flourishing of the Catholic Church.

THE ANALOGY OF MYSTERIES AND THEIR HIERARCHY

In the third and final part of this chapter we can consider the relation of the mysteries to one another according to analogy, that is to say, how they resemble one another even in the midst of their distinctness and how their unity amidst distinction is reflective of the eternal wisdom of God in his uncreated intelligence and goodness.

It is useful in this context first to recall two distinct notions of analogy found in Aquinas, even in the natural order of created being. One pertains to resemblances between effects and their cause, so that the effects resemble or are similar to their cause.[34] The properties of a substance (an individual human being), such as its quantity and qualities, each exist truly, but they exist in causal dependence on the ontologically prior entity of the substance in question.[35] For example the thinking of a human being and his free choices are qualifications of his being that stem from his more autonomous "core" or "center" of being, his subsistent personhood as a rational animal.

34. See on this point, Aquinas, *ST* I, q. 13, a. 5, and the study of John F. Wippel, "Thomas Aquinas on Our Knowledge of God and the Axiom that Every Agent Produces Something Like Itself," in *Metaphysical Themes in Thomas Aquinas II* (Washington, DC: The Catholic University of America Press, 2007), 152–71.
35. See Aquinas, *Commentary on Aristotle's* Metaphysics IV, lec. 1, 534–39, trans. J. P. Rowan (South Bend, IN: Dumb Ox Books, 1995).

Likewise, all created being resembles its transcendent source and origin, God, insofar as the latter is the Creator and communicator of
being to all that is outside of God.[36] This first form of analogy (resemblance of effects to their cause) is sometimes called the analogy
ad alterum since it refers us from one reality or set of configurations
in reality back to another that is causally antecedent.[37]

A second form of analogy is that which is sometimes termed the
"analogy of proper proportionality," and this is a likeness amidst difference found either between individual beings or between distinct
properties of individual beings, insofar as these each exist.[38] So for
example, two human beings can be said to truly exist or be good in
analogically similar ways, since their unique act of existence is distinct in each case and not essentially or generically the same, but still
somehow similar by analogy.[39] So likewise the various Aristotelian
"categories" of being indicate distinct genres of being—like quantity, quality, relation, and so forth—found in all things we experience.
Each of these "kinds" of metaphysical determinations exists in reality and is distinct (as quantities in things are really distinct from qualities or relations), but they all have existence, unity, intelligible truth,
and goodness (transcendental characteristics).[40] These transcendental characteristics are present in each genus of things and so "transcend" any one category or genus of being. They are only perceived
and apprehended analogically by us according to an analogy of proportion: A is to B as C is to D. Existence in quantity is similar to existence in quality, but the two modes of being are not reducible to

---

36. As Aquinas makes clear in *ST* I, q. 13, aa. 2 and 5.

37. I have explored elsewhere different forms of analogical attribution in Thomas
Joseph White, *Wisdom in the Face of Modernity: A Study in Thomistic Natural Theology*,
2nd ed. (Naples, FL: Sapientia Press, 2016).

38. See Aquinas, *De veritate*, q. 21, a. 1. In *Truth*, 3 vols, trans. J. V. McGlenn,
R. W. Mulligan, and R. W. Schmidt (Indianapolis, IN: Hackett, 1994).

39. See Aquinas, *De veritate*, q. 21, a. 2 and *Commentary on Aristotle's* Metaphysics,
IV, lec. 2, 561.

40. On the transcendentals see Aquinas, *De veritate*, q. 1, a. 1, and the study by
Jan Aertsen, *Medieval Philosophy and the Transcendentals: The Case of Thomas Aquinas*
(Leiden: Brill, 1996).

one another. The common "existence" is not grasped univocally but by a likeness that is analogical and distinctly transcendental in kind.

It is easy to see that we find something like these two kinds of analogy reproduced in the supernatural order, when we consider the relation of the various mysteries to one another. The relations of likeness and difference that then emerge help us grasp the unity and distinctness, as well as the hierarchy and global intelligibility of the mysteries of the Christian faith, as an expression of transcendent, uncreated divine wisdom.

The first form of analogy *ad alterum* or by reference to another in the order of causality, can readily be applied to the mysteries insofar as they are somehow derivative from another (in the order of ontological origin, or "efficient causality") or ordered to another (in the order of teleology or "final causality"). Here it is clear that the first and final locus of all orientation in Christian theology is the mystery of the Holy Trinity. The Holy Trinity is the primal mystery from which all things proceed and upon which they depend (in the order of metaphysical origination), and it is that mystery toward which all things are oriented, insofar as the universe generally, and spiritual creatures created in the image of God specifically, are divinely ordered by grace toward union with the uncreated Trinitarian life of God. From the Trinity and for the Trinity all things gain a kind of primal and ultimate intelligibility, one that is contemplated and explored in theological perspective.[41]

Emanations of theological causality reflective of the transcendent "logic" of divine wisdom and divine love then unfold from this primal Trinitarian point of reference. All of the creation derives from the Trinity. Internal to the visible creation there is a teleolog-

---

41. This is one reason why the *exitus-reditus* schema proposed by Marie-Dominique Chenu for interpreting the overarching order of the *Summa theologiae* in a Trinitarian way remains appealing to many. Chenu sees Aquinas organizing all theological topics in terms of an emanation and return ("exitus-reditus") from the Trinity to the Trinity. See likewise Jean-Hervé Nicolas, *Catholic Dogmatic Theology, A Synthesis, Book I, On the Trinitarian Mystery of God*, trans. M. K. Minerd (Washington, DC: The Catholic University of America Press, 2022).

ical summit: the human person is made in the image of the Trinity
and is created for grace and divine union.[42] The created person is
thus a principal and highest effect of the Trinity in the created order.[43] The Incarnation occurs within human history as a visible mission of the eternal Word of God and is seemingly enacted to redeem
the human race after the original rupture of the human race with
the grace of God.[44] The Eucharist and the other sacraments are instituted by Jesus of Nazareth, the Son of God made man, so they derive from the God-man. Likewise, the grace of Mary of Nazareth, the
historical Mother of God, is received by the Holy Trinity in view of
the Incarnation and the redemption, as well as the divine materni-
ty she exerts in the context of the life of the Catholic Church and its
members. The grace of Christ who is head of the Church is communicated to his members. Their life of grace and the cooperation they
undertake with Christ unfolds in and through the developmental
life of the Church. It culminates eschatologically in the life of glory
and beatitude, first for the souls of those who die in a state of grace,
and eventually for their bodies in the resurrection. We should notice
that in all these mysteries one can denote a divine intention of origins and ends. What emerges from this portrait is a mystical chain
of causality, in which the supernatural mysteries made known to us
by way of revelation alone are seen to entail an ordering wisdom of
divine origination and divine purpose, in which the economic work
of God unfolds from Trinitarian initiatives in view of Trinitarian ac-
complishments. Everything is from the Trinity and for the Trinity.

We can see in this light how the second kind of analogy, according to proper proportionality, might unfold as an effect of the first.
Because the supernatural mysteries of Christianity come forth from

42. Aquinas, *ST* I, q. 93.

43. See the Second Vatican Council, Pastoral Constitution on the Church in the
Modern World, *Gaudium et spes*, §12: "For Sacred Scripture teaches that man was creat-
ed 'to the image of God,' as able to know and love his creator, over all earthly creatures
(Gen. 1:26; Wis. 2:23) that he might rule them, and make use of them, while glorifying
God."

44. See the argument to this effect by Aquinas on the motive of the Incarnation in
ST III, q. 1, aa. 1 and 3.

one another in view of a common end, they resemble one another intrinsically. As A is to B, so C is to D, or as the divine wisdom is manifest in one supernatural mystery in one way, so it is manifest in another mystery in another way by similitude. So for example, if (A) is taken to symbolize the wisdom of God refracted in the Incarnation (B), then it is similar to and dissimilar to the wisdom of God indicated by (C), which is refracted in the Eucharist (D). The mysteries have similar notes of wisdom or divine intelligibility, so that when we study them, we come to see likenesses of the divine transcendent wisdom and of the loving order that emanates from that wisdom.

Of course the similitudes in question are not those of either created metaphysical genera or created transcendentals. The likenesses in question are properly supernatural and numinous, not reducible to the mere horizon of natural metaphysical reason, but there is something in common between the two "registers" of analogy: that which pertains to the natural order of metaphysical likeness and that which pertains to the supernatural order of mystery (by real ontological similitude of the natural to the supernatural). Of course in saying this we are in no way claiming that the natural order of analogy either anticipates or can be employed to derive intrinsic knowledge of the supernatural order but only that in the light of the entirely gratuitous and previously unknown revelation of the supernatural, there appears then and thereafter (only post facto) the similitude of the natural order (in some respects only) to the supernatural order, and then only numinously and amidst irreducible dissimilitudes.

We may think here of the five distinct mysteries we have chosen above insofar as they in some way resemble or are integrally related to one another. The notion of the persons of the Trinity understood as subsistent relations is indicative of the mystery that each person is wholly relative to the others in all that he is and is truly distinct from the others, even as he is truly the one God. The Son of God, then, is eternally begotten of the Father as his eternal Word, God from God, light from light, true God from true God, related to the Father in all that he is as the Son, wholly from the Father in all that he is, and himself wholly and truly God, possessing in himself from the Father the plenitude of the perfection of divine life and being.

It is this same Son of God who is made man in virtue of the Incarnation. The notion of the hypostatic union (our second mystery) indicates that the person of the Son subsists truly in two natures in such a way that he is one in being and person, even as he is truly God and truly man. The eternal relation that characterizes him personally as the Son of the Father is thus instantiated and manifest in his concrete historical humanity. The historical figure Jesus of Nazareth, as depicted in the New Testament Gospels, is filial in all he is, related personally to the Father as the one from whom he comes forth and to whom he is related, in all his actions and sufferings as man, as well as in his resurrection. The human life of Jesus is thus a human display or epiphany of the personal relation of the Son to the Father, albeit in a human mode.

The Eucharist is the conversion of the substance of bread and wine, respectively, into the body and blood of the glorified Christ. As such it presupposes the historical resurrection of Christ in his human nature, so that he is now glorified forever in both body and soul. In the Eucharist, the change of the substance of bread into his body and of wine into his blood renders truly present the substance of the glorified Christ. Since his body and blood are present, so too his soul and divinity are present by concomitance. The economy of the Son's redemption continues then in the Eucharistic presence, under the accidents of bread and wine, and the grace of Christ crucified is communicated in the celebration of the Mass to the members of Christ's faithful. There the person of the Son is numinously present, formally in his human nature, and thus also in his divine person, and so the Trinity is revealed among us in a Eucharistic mode. The grace of the sacrifice of his redemption is applied to the life of the faithful and animates the inward life of members of the Church.

In the mystery of sanctifying grace, the grace and life of Christ in his sacred humanity (the life of his soul as man) is shared with Christians and communicated from him and by him to them so that they become members of his mystical body. In receiving grace into the essence of their souls, they are not transformed into the individual Christ (substantially) but are changed by a radically qualifying accident or property of the human person, so as to live in habitual spiritual health, by what Thomists have called an entitative habitus. In such a way they live in friendship with God in grace, exercising the new divine life within them principally by means of the infused theological virtues, the infused moral virtues, and the gifts of the Holy Spirit.

The life of grace in individuals and in the Church collectively grows and develops over time. Insofar as this life has an intellectual dimension and self-expression, it has an external expression in teaching, theological reflection, and in the official doctrinal development of the Church. Just as life grows, is nourished, defends itself, and is fruitful, so too the intellectual life of the Church is expressed in this way, organically in continuity, in the assimilation of new modes of expression, in self-defense from error and in view of clarification, and in the service of charity, holiness, and the greater growth of the universal communion of the Church. The orientation of this life of development of the Church and its doctrinal self-expression is eschatological in orientation. The Church is in pilgrimage throughout history and in its own developmental life in view of the fulfillment of the end times and the glorified life of the world to come, which will also transform the earthly life of humanity and the cosmos. The assimilation of all things is unto the Trinity and in view of the participation in and enjoyment of Trinitarian life.

We can note that the mysteries designated in themselves individually resemble one another and are related to one another by a supernatural causal connection that in turn reflects a divine wisdom and a divine goodness. Moving backward up the chain of origination from the last to the first, we can say that the developmental life of the Church presupposes the infusion of the life of grace from Christ into our humanity. This infusion of grace presupposes the sacramental economy and especially the Eucharistic celebration. The Eucharist

and the other sacraments presuppose the mystery of the hypostatic union (the Incarnation), and the hypostatic union presupposes
the primal mystery of the Most Holy Trinity (which we denote by
speaking of subsistent relations and eternal processions in God). If
we change the direction of reasoning and move from the first to the
last, we can say that from the eternal Trinity there is an unfolding
of the Trinitarian economy in creation and redemption. This is expressed in the mysteries of the Incarnation, the Eucharist, the life of
grace, and the life of the Church. The Church in her membership is
oriented back to the Trinity as the final end of all things, by way of
divinization, which is itself the culmination of the creation.

Finally, this analogical and causal perspective allows us to understand the concept of the hierarchy of mysteries, which is related logically to the notion of the hierarchy of truths.[45] Mysteries are
"higher" in the hierarchical order of truth when they are more primal in the order of causation and thus in the order of supernatural explanation. The Trinity is the most primal of all mysteries, that
which casts the most ultimate intelligible light upon all others. The
Incarnation is closely allied to it, not because it is the first of all mysteries in the order of the economy (the creation of the invisible and
visible worlds precedes it, as does the communication of grace and
the fall of angels and human beings, as well as the eventual election
of Israel). Instead the Incarnation is closest because it represents the
summit of revelation—given to creatures within the economy—of
the inner life of the Most Holy Trinity. The Incarnation and Paschal
Mystery of Christ is the culminating moment in the visible mission

45. See the Second Vatican Council, Decree on Ecumenism, *Unitatis redintegratio*,
§11, on the hierarchy of truths. See the essay by E. J. Echeverria, "Hierarchy of Truths
Revisited," published in *African Journals Online (AJOL)* (2015): 11–35; https://www.ajol
.info//index.php/actat/article/view/146057. As Echeverria notes, following many other theologians, all revealed teachings stem from God's self-manifestation, and therefore,
one is obliged in faith to accept them, even if they are hierarchically arranged in relation
to one other. This fact suggests the deepest reason for the hierarchy, as we are seeking to
indicate here: the hierarchy is ultimately explained ontologically by reference to causality
and the analogy of faith. Mysteries are more central and unoriginate or more remote and
derivative. Yet they all arise from God in their distinctness and inter-relation, rather than
from the constructions of human religious tradition or our anthropological subjectivity.

of the Word of God, in whom the Father expresses himself outwardly in creation, even in our created human nature, so as to send the Holy Spirit to induct us divinely and supernaturally into the inner life of God himself. The Eucharist, meanwhile, is instituted by the Son of God made man and so it depends upon him, temporally and ontologically. Metaphysically speaking, it is possible for the Incarnation to take place without the Eucharist, but it is not possible for the Eucharist to take place without the Incarnation. However, in another sense, the Eucharist just is the Incarnation, insofar as it is the sacramental presence of the Incarnate Son of God in his glorified humanity, rendered present through sacred signs (accidental properties of bread and wine) and in the very substance of his body and blood. Likewise the grace of Christians and the developmental life of the grace of the Church come from Christ himself, in his sacred humanity, and depend upon him. Christ is a more primary mystery and causal reality in the order of revelation and of salvation than the Church is. And yet, because Christ is, and because his grace is truly present in the creation, so too the Church is real and is the vehicle for his self-revelation and communication of divine life to the world.

Truths about God's revelation that are derivative from other truths, or secondary in their ontological foundations, are not for this reason less ontologically real or veridical. In one sense the opposite is the case, insofar as the denial of a derivative truth (such as the reality of supernatural grace) could lead readily to the denial of a more primal mystery of origin (such as the reality of the hypostatic union or that of the Trinity itself). To believe in the most primary and ultimate of all mysteries (God the Trinity) is to believe in all that unfolds and descends from the Trinitarian life of God, as expressed in the Church and in her universal expression of faith. The Church's theological tradition serves to trace out the inward order and logic of God's transcendent wisdom as it is manifest in the mysteries, so as to familiarize the children of God supernaturally with the inward mystery of God himself, as he expresses his hidden Trinitarian identity in his manifold supernatural works.

CONCLUSION

The study of the nexus of mysteries is only one part of Catholic theology, as we have noted in the previous chapter. And yet it is the
principal part, insofar as theology is concerned with the mystery of
God in himself and with the doctrinal formulations of the Church
and the inward content of supernatural mystery that they signify.
Historical study of the development of doctrines (in scripture, patristic and medieval thought, and amidst modern controversies, debates, and clarifications) can concern itself especially with the con-
tingencies of historical opinion and the outcomes of significant
doctrinal debates in the body politic of the Catholic religion. Such
historical study of the teaching of the Church and its development
has an essential place in Catholic intellectual life. However the terminus even of such historically nuanced inquiry is found ultimately
in true judgment regarding the inward structure of Christian mystery, in regard to God and his activity in creation, particularly in the
supernatural mysteries that reveal him in an especially ultimate way.
This is why theologians who concern themselves with the inward
character of mysteries and with the analogy of the mysteries to one
another, as well as their originating explanations and final purposes,
are those who preserve the theological tradition of the Church in
the most profound way, and it is their intellectual explorations that
are typically the most perduring through time. They are also those
theologians whose work accords most perfectly with the contemplative and spiritual aspiration of the Christian spiritual life, since
the latter aspires to union with God by knowledge and love. A theology of the mysteries has a commensurate goal, since it aims to elevate the gaze of the Christian toward the consideration of God in
himself, so that God may be more deeply understood in this life by
faith and by love, and so that the Christian heart ultimately may
burn with the sight of uncreated glory.

3

On Theology as *Sacra Doctrina*

Catholic Theology, The Pluralism of Catholic Schools, and the Ecumenical Aspect of Catholic Theology

If the truth of divine revelation is one, why are there diverse theological understandings of that revelation? Do these follow only from the limitation, partiality, and diversity of viewpoints of human beings, and if so, how is the unity of the confession of the Catholic faith maintained across time? Or is the truth of the faith itself somehow so ineluctably transcendent that it can hardly be uttered or understood across time and place in any unified way? If pluralism in Catholic theology poses important problems, so does the existence of schools of thought, such as that of Thomism, as distinct from, say, Scotism, or the modern "Communio" school that takes inspiration from authors like Henri de Lubac, Joseph Ratzinger, and Hans Urs von Balthasar. But perhaps it is even an artifice and a superficial notion when one speaks of such schools to refer obliquely to diverse figures in history not subject to easy categorization. And what is the role of philosophy in this mix of questions, since there are a number of diverse philosophical theses in Christian intellectual history that affect the stances authors take in their diverse theological undertakings, as they speak not only about philosophy but about the mystery of God, making use of philosophy? Last of all, what is the relation of this kind of problem of pluralism *within* Catholic theology when one compares it with non-Catholic Christian theology, such as that of Protestant theologians, especially those such as Karl Barth, or in his own way, G. W. F. Hegel, who have greatly influenced conversations in modern Catholic theology? My aim below is not to treat such questions comprehensively, which would not be possible for many reasons, but rather to underscore some signal points of reference for a sound understanding of the practice of Catholic theology as *sacra doctrina*, the study of the revealed mystery of God, as it is related to philosophy and ecumenism. I will relate my comments in particular to the contrasting figure of Karl Barth at points, since Barth's view of theology as a form of thought distinct from and outside of philosophical metaphysics (including metaphysical reflection on God) stands in vivid contrast to the tradition of St. Thomas and to mainstream Catholic theology more generally, but there are also important points of contact between Aquinas and Barth that are worthy of mention and that help one consider in greater detail the possibility of ecumenical exchange between Catholic and Protestant theologians seeking in diverse ways to speak of the mystery of God and of Christ, as well as of other key themes in dogmatic theology.

SACRA DOCTRINA

At the start of our reflections on the topic of Catholic unity of the truth and legitimate theological pluralism, it is important to make a few comments about Thomistic self-understanding regarding the practice of theology as a normative discipline and how it relates to Scripture, Tradition, dogma, and philosophy, as well as normative claims about orthodoxy and heresy. As anyone recognizes, Aquinas is of central importance in the Catholic tradition, but is also only one theologian among many. Evidently, no one who is a member of the Catholic Church is required intellectually to be committed to Thomistic interpretations of commonly held doctrine, let alone to Aquinas's own distinctive philosophy. What then do Catholic Thomists make, methodologically, of the inherent theological pluralism within their own Church, and how does it relate to argumentative claims Thomists sometimes propose regarding the supposed insufficiencies of alternative theological viewpoints or the conceptual advantages of Thomistic positions in Catholic theology?

First let us simply note some levels of authority that Aquinas himself recognizes in question 1 of *Summa theologiae* [*ST*] I and questions 1–2 of *ST* I-II. My list below is affected by an interpretation of Aquinas made in light of the Second Vatican Council's Dogmatic Constitution on Divine Revelation, *Dei Verbum*, but it is not for that reason, I think, artificial or extrinsically imposed.

(1) God reveals himself in free self-disclosure and self-communication by way of grace, teaching us through the medium of the prophets and apostles, and this teaching is found in Scripture and early apostolic Tradition. It is received, transmitted, and understood within the living tradition of the Church. The whole Church is assisted by the Holy Spirit in this process to understand and receive the teaching of God revealed in Christ faithfully down through the ages, not without the assistance of the apostolic college, that is to say, the episcopal authorities of the Church acting in communion with the see of Rome.

(2) This teaching is itself codified at times in dogmatic universal pronouncements, which are not identical with primal revelation as such but which seek to promote and protect right understandings of integral elements of it. The dogmatic teaching of the Council of Chalcedon, for example, is not identical with scriptural revelation but is taken to indicate something perennially true about the being of Christ that is revealed implicitly in the New Testament. Most Catholic theologians agree that the Church understands this kind of dogmatic teaching as infallibly expressive of divine revelation and irreformable. This does not mean that the teachings given in these locales are comprehensive or fully adequate, but they do indicate

core confessional truths, manifest implicitly or explicitly in Scripture, which must be preserved through the ages, even if such conciliar teachings also can be reinterpreted in various ways in subsequent ages *in new theological and philosophical formats.* The latter formats, novel though they may be in each age, need to preserve sufficiently the acquisitions of the Church's previous claims. This includes whatever is essential in the ontological content of the classical dogmatic tradition.[1] Of course theologians working with the magisterium of the Church try to work out over time what is essential in the ontological signification of the past teachings as they are interpreted within the horizon of new contexts.

(3) There are different schools of theology within the Catholic Church, for example, Augustinian, Syriac, Byzantine Eastern Catholic, Bonaventurian, Thomist, Scotist, Suarezian, Rahnerian, Balthasarian, and so on. This is not a comprehensive list. *These distinct schools of thought all have a common commitment to the two levels indicated above: divine revelation and its doctrinal formulations.* They are united within the Church by this common confession of faith and come to distinct interpretations of that revelation. It is true that sometimes members of one of these schools argue that the position of another school leads implicitly toward a heretical position inadvertently. Aquinas seems to have thought this about Alexander of Hales's theology, as leading inadvertently toward a problematic form of Nestorianism, for example. And I think this about Rahner's Christology, as I have argued elsewhere.[2] More often, however, they accuse them of being wrong theologically, which is not an identical charge. Neither of these forms of argumentation entails the accusation of heresy of course. Heresy amounts to a willful defense of a teaching condemned by the Catholic Church or the willful denial of

---

1. One may think here of John Henry Newman's explorations on the topic of the continuity that takes place in the development of doctrine, and of Yves Congar's understanding of actualizing tradition in *Tradition and Traditions* (*La tradition et les traditions*, 2 vols. [Paris: A. Fayard, 1960–1963]).

2. See White, *The Incarnate Lord*, ch. 1.

a proposition taught by the Church. By contrast, theological error is something most theologians traffic in at some time, perhaps even daily, despite their best intentions, and has to do with the struggle to understand the truth of revelation within diverse traditions, some of which may promote less perfect, erroneous, or deficient understandings. Of course some also think that the various positions of major schools each have it partly right or are mostly compatible and convergent toward a mutual understanding of a given mystery, or are equally inadequate. A Scotist Trinitarian theologian, for example, may argue that the Thomistic view of the persons in the Trinity as subsistent relations is incoherent. In response, a Thomist can argue to the contrary that the Scotistic view of the Trinitarian persons is problematically univocalist, that is, erroneous. But a Thomist who declares the Scotist to be doctrinally outside the Catholic Church for this view is not speaking reasonably. Instead, both are arguing about the actual content of what they already agree on (the dogmatic confession of Trinitarian faith) but have distinct and partially incompatible accounts of that content. I take it that Barthians and Thomists are often doing something analogous, if not precisely identical (since Barthians are not Catholic, typically, and believe in reformable dogmatic ecclesial claims).

(4) How do distinct philosophies relate to the distinct schools? It is true that distinct philosophical views emerge among various theologians and their followers. Aquinas famously believes in the real distinction and composition of essence and existence in all creatures and in its non-distinction in God, a view Scotus and Suárez each reject in distinct ways. Aquinas's view on this point has many implications for his theology of creation, the Trinity, and the hypostatic union. Henry of Ghent and Scotus, meanwhile, have irreconcilable anthropological notions of the way human beings formulate concepts, and they make use of these distinct ideas in their reflections on the eternal Son as the *Verbum* of God. Von Balthasar and Rahner differ deeply on the nature of anthropology, natural knowledge of God, and the possibility of metaphysics in a post-Kantian

setting. What should we make of all this diversity that is so deeply interrelated to the diverse "philosophies" used within theology?

First, differences among the schools do not arise only or even primarily from their respective philosophies. *They arise from different conceptions of the truth about the mystery of revelation itself.* That is to say, differences of opinion in various schools arise principally from diverse conceptions of the formal objects of faith as such (i.e., from diverse conceptions of the Trinity or Incarnation or other mysteries) rather than the philosophical instruments of *sacra doctrina.*

That being said, differences among the schools do arise *in part* due to distinct philosophical commitments. Scotus and Ockham come to very distinct views of the Trinity and the psychological analogy in part because of the ways they understand divine simplicity, which are related in turn to their metaphysical views about composition in creatures and the truths we can infer about God from those compositions.[3]

On this view, there is no point in Catholic theological history at which non-Christian philosophical ideas were taken up into the practice of theology uncritically, without being discussed, vetted, reformulated, and reconsidered in light of Christ and the New Testament revelation. The use of *ousia* metaphysics by Church Fathers in the fourth century, for example, entailed a reformation of ambient philosophical concepts in view of the exposition of a distinctively Christian, Trinitarian confession of faith at Nicaea.[4] The medieval project of trying to understand philosophical notions in Aristotle or Avicenna within a Christian context (substance, relation, and so forth) took place overtly by critique of these philosophical concepts, conducted in light of Christ and the apostolic Tradition. This was the main point of the dispute of how to critically receive and evalu-

3. See the study of Russell L. Friedman, *Medieval Trinitarian Thought from Aquinas to Ockham* (Cambridge: Cambridge University Press, 2013).

4. See for example the helpful analysis of Khaled Anatolios, *Retrieving Nicaea: The Development and Meaning of Trinitarian Doctrine* (Grand Rapids, MI: Baker Academic, 2018), and Brian Daley, *God Visible: Patristic Christology Reconsidered* (Oxford: Oxford University press, 2018).

ate the Aristotelian heritage in the high Middle Ages.[5] The modern Catholic use of the classical terms like "essence," "person," "relation," and "nature" in creedal formulations retains a decidedly ontological signification, but distinct schools of thought interpret in varied ways how we might best preserve their use. Many modern Catholic theologians seek to preserve classical ontological significations while transposing them into modern philosophical idioms. Walter Kasper, for example, has quite impressively sought to make use of ideas from both F. W. J. Schelling and the Frankfurt school to articulate a commitment to classical Nicene-Chalcedonian dogma in modern ontological idioms.[6] Rahner seeks to do something analogous in developing his own Thomistic version of transcendental anthropology.[7]

We should note three sub-presuppositions latent in what has been argued up to this point:

First, Catholics can agree with Protestants at least in some ways when the latter claim that, as regards the use of philosophical metaphysics, "there is never any nature that does not presuppose grace": philosophical reflection in the Catholic theological tradition presupposes always already an ongoing reformation of all prior philosophical notions in light of Christ. This is not a novel view, as any historian of patristic or medieval theology should rightly attest.[8]

5. See on this point the analysis of Russell L. Friedman in *Intellectual Traditions at the Medieval University: The Use of Philosophical Psychology in Trinitarian Theology among the Franciscans and Dominicans, 1250–1350*, 2 vols. (Leiden: Brill, 2012).

6. See Walter Kasper, *The God of Jesus Christ*, trans. M. J. O'Connell (New York: Crossroad, 1989).

7. Karl Rahner, *Foundations of Christian Faith: An Introduction to the Idea of Christianity*, trans. W. V. Dych (New York: Seabury, 1978).

8. If one presses this argument from the Barthian side, so as to claim that there are no merely philosophical notions in an authentic Christian theology, it can become self-defeating. Let us agree that the grace of Christ and his covenant is the backbone of the creation, such that all that is given in creation is always already given from, for, and unto the mystery of the covenant of grace. This entails, in Barth's logic, that all natural unfolding of creation is in some way anticipated by and taken up into the dynamic history of election. By this very measure it becomes possible conceptually to posit that, "because grace is everywhere" in human culture, human culture will have evolved naturally under grace, so as to anticipate and be able to signify *something of the reality of God naturally*, only after and from the effects of grace. If by a "doctrine of lights" one presses

Second and simultaneously, grace does presuppose nature: there are no philosophically innocent theologians. Every theologian makes some use of philosophical and indeed metaphysical notions, whether modern or classical, even if he or she also seeks to baptize them within a theological format, as presumably Barth has tried to do (however successful one thinks he is) with Kant and Hegel, or Schleiermacher with his modern metaphysics of consciousness, or Eberhard Jüngel with Heidegger. I take it that none of these thinkers operates without at least an implicit commitment to philosophical and metaphysical positions, and none can rightly be understood without some philosophical analysis as such. On this view, there is no epistemic possibility of a post-metaphysical theology. Instead, each theologian is bound to take up some option among alternative metaphysical influences.

Third, all this need not lead to the conclusion that medieval theology and metaphysics in general or Thomism in particular must represent the apex of an intellectually informed faith. The idea that "older is better" or "newer is better" is misleading. What is best is what is true, not what appears in time either earlier or later.

Where does this leave us? Based on the account I am offering, there is no tradition free from a philosophically influenced reading of the New Testament and the patristic tradition. New Testament exegetes and Protestant theologians who interpret St. Paul's ontology in relational terms may well be influenced by the Barthian tradition, and by that very measure, I think one can perceive in such interpretations some effect of Hegel's *Logic* in the rendering of relation in Paul. That does not mean that Barth's relational analysis of covenant in Paul is erroneous, but it does mean that we should treat skeptically any claim of Protestant theologians to provide us with chemically pure interpretations of Scripture that are free from the taint of or

the idea that cultures "outside" the historical sphere of overt Christian confession can anticipate something (anything) of the truth about God, then one is very close to a form of thinking compatible in principle with the First Vatican Council. In the light of grace and divine revelation, it becomes clear to us that we are naturally capable of thinking about God the Creator, whom we now know in Christ as the Triune God.

dependence on frameworks of reception through the medium of a theological tradition that has itself assimilated philosophy (however critically or uncritically).

Neither Schleiermacher's nor Barth's use of post-Kantian ontological categories indicates a theological problem per se, based on what I have mentioned above. As I have argued elsewhere, a Catholic theologian can think of Barth in particular as a helpful resource for thinking about how to express many biblical and traditional Christian claims in a distinctively modern context and idiom.[9] If one interprets him as successfully "modern and orthodox" on various points of theology (for example in his articulation of elements of Chalcedonian Christology), this does not make him better or worse than Athanasius or Aquinas, but it means we have a right and responsibility to compare them among themselves and with others to think about what we take to be the best formulations ontologically, in light of Tradition and in accord with Scripture and common doctrine (like Chalcedon), as well as sound philosophical practices.

This being said, theologians should generally treat the acquisitions of the great Tradition as having a greater weight than lone innovations, if only because the popularity of the "common doctors" suggests, by their widespread acceptance and use, the possibility of a greater accord with the *sensus fidei* of all the baptized. Augustine is a reference in part because he helps us get to the Church's common thinking regarding the truth of divine revelation, and he does so by making constructive use of the ambient pre-Christian philosophical heritage. The same could be said of many notable theological "doctors" of the past. This means that newer ideas should, as John Henry Newman said, be subject to assessment by association with the various references of the Tradition in those instances where the latter display "chronic vigor."[10]

---

9. See Thomas Joseph White, "The Crucified Lord: Thomistic Reflections on the Communication of Idioms and the Theology of the Cross," in *Aquinas and Barth: An Unofficial Catholic Protestant Ecumenical Dialogue* (Grand Rapids, MI: Eerdmans, 2013), 157–92.

10. John Henry Newman, *An Essay On Development Of Christian Doctrine* (Notre

There is admittedly an outstanding difference between Barth and the Catholic tradition at least on this point: whether the Christian critique and reformation of all non-Christian forms of ontology may give rise to a "philosophy on Christian soil," or a Christian philosophy, that is fully assimilated to and compatible with the scriptural deposit of faith and the dogmatic Tradition but susceptible in principle to extraction for the purposes of teaching philosophy (or metaphysics) as a distinct field of reflection.[11] *After Christ and in his light* is it possible for there to be a philosophical metaphysics as such? Concretely speaking, can one teach a class of philosophy in a seminary that offers metaphysical analysis of what a living thing is, or a human person, or philosophical arguments for the existence of God, and so on? Here Catholic theologians most typically hold that such philosophical instances of thought are possible and even salutary, especially given the effects of sin (original, personal, collective) on human intellectual endeavors outside of the realm of grace. Due to the effects of sin and the need for grace, non-Christians may be unlikely to interest themselves in or accept such a Christian philosophy, but if grace presupposes and must heal and rehabilitate nature in the light of Christ, then some re-formation in philosophy is necessary even on—and especially on—Christian soil.[12] Relatedly, the Catholic Church teaches that there are *praeambula fidei*, philosophical and moral truths accessible to reason in principle but difficult to attain to in our fallen state, that the Church teaches authoritatively (so that they can be known by all), but that are philosophical as

---

Dame, IN: University of Notre Dame Press, 1989). Chronic vigor is the seventh of the famous seven notes of authentic development.

11. I take it as a matter of historical fact, on this point, that Aquinas for example does think that there are philosophical demonstrations of the existence of God. See Lawrence Dewan, "The Existence of God: Can It Be Demonstrated?," *Nova et Vetera* (English edition) 10, no. 3 (2012): 731–56.

12. There are famous twentieth-century disputes on the nature of Christian philosophy, a concept that appears in the papal encyclical *Fides et ratio* (John Paul II, Encyclical Letter *Fides et ratio* [September 14, 1998]). I propose ways of thinking about this theme that take some inspiration from Jacques Maritain in an appendix of my book *Wisdom in the Face of Modernity*, 2nd ed. (Naples, FL: Sapientia Press, 2016).

such.[13] She also teaches that there are "reasons of credibility," derived from signs of the truth of revelation, in things like ongoing miracles or the moral witness of the saints, which designate obliquely the truth of the Christian faith to human reason in *extrinsic* ways that do not provide the grace of faith as such but that do show forth publicly its rationality or non-irrationality.

This last point does remain an outstanding topic of division between Catholics and many Protestants, but how important is it? I will now turn to the question of philosophical theology as it affects ecumenical theology, specifically in exchanges between Catholic and Protestant theologians.

THE *ANALOGIA ENTIS* AND ECUMENICAL THEOLOGY

Clearly the engagement between Erich Przywara and Karl Barth in the early 1930s was an occasion of elevated ecumenical encounter and gave rise to subsequent conversations of great importance, not least in virtue of von Balthasar's famous book, *The Theology of Karl Barth*, as well as in many other instances.[14] Nevertheless, we should ask ourselves whether either Przywara or Barth rightly identified the theologically essential differences between Protestantism and Catholicism. Is Barth correct to say, for example, in *Church Dogmatics* (*CD*) I/1 (*Doctrine of the Word of God*, part 1) that the use of the *analogia entis* presents the identifying characteristic of Catholic thought?[15]

I would like to suggest two errors that were made in this debate and refer to one intervention that acts as a remedy. The first error as I see it, and perhaps the most consequential, stems from Przywara,

13. First Vatican Council, *Dei Filius*; 1992 *Catechism of the Catholic Church*, §§36–38.

14. Hans Urs von Balthasar, *The Theology of Karl Barth: Exposition and Interpretation*, trans. E. Oakes (San Francisco: Ignatius Press, 1992).

15. See Karl Barth, *Church Dogmatics*, trans. G. W. Bromiley and T. F. Torrance, vol. I/1 (London: T&T Clark; New York: Continuum, 2004), xiii: "I regard the *analogia entis* as the invention of Antichrist, and I believe that because of it it is impossible ever to become a Catholic."

who famously claimed that the *analogia entis* is the "fundamental form of Catholic theology."[16] When most Catholics speak, admittedly somewhat vaguely, of an *analogia entis*, they mean to refer to the human ability to know something of God by way of natural philosophical reflection. (Incidentally, this is how I almost always use the term as well.) Przywara does not mean this alone however, as John Betz has repeatedly and rightly pointed out.[17] Importantly, Przywara's definition includes philosophical knowledge of God by way of metaphysical reflection and analogical discourse. However, this form of knowledge is itself, for Przywara, taken up into a larger Catholic thought-form that includes properly theological reflection on the mystery of the Trinity and Christ, as well as the Virgin Mary, the Church, and the sacraments. In fact he is referring by this term to ontological similitudes between the Trinity and creatures that emerge in a variety of instances, in the rhythm of creation (characterized in part by the metaphysics of the real distinction of *esse* and *essentia*), by the history of human beings under grace, by the Incarnation in the two natures of Christ, by the fiat in grace of the Virgin Mary, and by the life of the Church in the Holy Spirit.[18]

What is significant for our purposes is that Przywara claimed that the study of this structure of ontological similitude, evinced in the orders of both nature and grace and known philosophically and theologically, is the essence of Catholic theology. If I understand him rightly this means that the essence or formal object of Catholic thought is the study of the similitudes between the Trinity and creatures, making use of a sound metaphysics. He contrasts this, in turn, with what he takes to be "essential" to Protestantism, a distrust of human mediations, behind which Przywara posits a latent oppo-

16. See the expression of this idea as expressed after his debate with Barth in Erich Przywara, *Analogia Entis: Metaphysics: Original Structure and Universal Rhythm*, trans. J. Betz and D. B. Hart (Grand Rapids, MI: Eerdmans, 2014), 348–99 (pt. 2, ch. 2: "The Scope of Analogy as a Fundamental Catholic Form").

17. See John R. Betz, "Erich Przywara and Karl Barth: On the *Analogia Entis* as a Formal Principle of Catholic Theology," in *The Analogy of Being: Invention of the Antichrist or Wisdom of God?*, ed. T. J. White (Grand Rapids, MI: Eerdmans, 2011), 35–87.

18. See Przywara, *Analogia Entis: Metaphysics*, 185–91, 234–37, 493, for example.

sitional mode of thinking between God as sovereign agent and the human agency of persons, their natural powers even under grace, their cooperation in the order of sanctification, and so forth.[19] One suspects he is suggesting that there is an implicit meta-ontology that lies behind the doctrine of justification in Luther's early theology, which is reflected in the subsequent Lutheran and Reformed refusal of various facets of the Catholic tradition, such as instances of authoritative doctrinal clarification, Mariology, theories of instrumental sacramental theology, and so forth.

Przywara's ideas are interesting and perfectly appropriate to explore within the context of a robust ecumenical conversation. However, it seems to me that he in fact misled Barth by his characterization of the "fundamental form" or essence of Catholic theology. Let us return to our consideration of *sacra doctrina* from the first part of this chapter. What is the formal object of Catholic theology? Medieval theologians expended great effort arguing about this topic, presenting diverse theories, some saying Christ the Word made human (the Incarnation), others saying the Church's life and her sacraments.[20] Aquinas's view is that the proper object of theology is God the Holy Trinity.[21] The essence of theology pertains primarily, then, to the study of God, revealed in Christ. Based on this view of *sacra doctrina*, Aquinas stipulates in turn that one must understand all things in light of the Trinity, which is why the Nicene-Constantinopolitan Creed functions as a reference for core principles, as it allows us to read Scripture correctly in a Trinitarian light, and interpret the scriptural revelation in a Trinitarian perspective.[22]

What none of the medievals—or any one else before or since Przywara—has ever claimed is that the formal object of theology is the study of the ontological similitudes between the Trinity and the creation. That is not a ridiculous suggestion, and indeed it

---

19. Przywara, *Analogia Entis: Metaphysics*, 348–53.

20. See Ulrich G. Leinsle, *Introduction to Scholastic Theology*, trans. M. J. Miller (Washington, DC: The Catholic University of America Press, 2010), 120–81.

21. Thomas Aquinas, *ST* I, q. 1; II-II, q. 1, a. 1.

22. *ST* I, q. 1, a. 7.

has some potential connections to Aquinas, as I have just intimated. We should note, however, the difference. In Aquinas it is clear that theology "looks" first and foremost at the Trinity and interprets the world in light of the ultimate truth revealed in Scripture, making some measured use of philosophical ontology within theology. Przywara seems to invert the order of procession; the philosophical study of the analogy of being, which has roots in Greek philosophy, anticipates a rhythm of being we will discover again at a higher level, in the domain of revealed truths about Trinitarian ontology. It may be possible to defend his claim from a Thomistic point of view, but what Przywara does by his approach is to give us the impression that if we first begin with the right metaphysics we can eventually attain to the right theology.[23] The study of philosophical ontology inaugurates the engagement with revelation itself.

Barth's reaction is equally nebulous or disputable, to my mind. It seems clear enough that the classical disputes stemming from the Reformation era are about mediation: is there an episcopal structure stemming from apostolic times that is an essential part of the constitution of the Church? Are there seven sacraments, or only two, and what is a sacrament? In what sense is it a sign and instrument of grace, or is it? Can Church councils be said to formulate irreformable, infallible doctrines that are free from error, and in what sense is it true to say that the Church preserves infallible teaching? Are the Virgin Mary and the "saints" exemplars of the life of grace, whose actions under cooperative grace manifest the saving power of Christ's action in the world, or is this Catholic superstructure an extrinsic scaffolding obscuring the true face of Christ? The Reformation "solas" regarding Scripture, justification by faith alone, and grace alone (meaning God acting prior to and above human cooperation) work to assure a more restricted view of mediation, presumably in view of the greater manifestation of the glory of God alone and the centrality of Christ as the unique mediator of salvation.

23. Perhaps his idea could be restated in a more measured way: "Without a realistic sense of philosophical ontology one will not be able to cooperate well with the articulation of the theological mystery." Yet his view seems to go further than this.

Many classical Lutheran, Reformed, and Anglican theologians reserve a place for the measured use of philosophy within dogmatics, including philosophical arguments as such for the existence of God and the determination of what we might say or not say about his attributes. Barth presented the rather novel claim in *CD* I/1, however, that the *core differences* between Catholic and Protestant theology stem from the *analogia entis*, initially interpreted largely as "natural theology," which then creeps into every facet of Catholic theology.[24]

This is, historically speaking, a very novel claim. It may be defensible, especially if one thinks that Przywara's account of the *analogia entis* as "the fundamental form of theology" in the Catholic tradition is correct. However, Przywara's claim amounts to nothing more than a very brilliant and eccentric thought experiment, one held by virtually no one before him or since. But Barth takes it as insightful and constructs a counter-reaction, which is somewhat similar in content but distinct in method.

It is distinct in method because the fundamental core of Reformed theology, according to Barth, is determined by knowledge of God procured only by revelation and only by the consistent activity of the Holy Spirit, without *any* contribution from philosophy. We should note the dialectical reaction here: if Przywara suggested that philosophical metaphysics set the tone for Catholic theology as a kind of initiation, Barth reacts by denying any role to specifically philosophical or metaphysical knowledge of God as such even *within sacra doctrina*. Neither of these positions seems to reflect that of

24. See Barth on the *analogia entis* in *CD* I/2 (London: T&T Clark, 1963), 144–46, esp. 144–45:

E. Przywara purports to give us final clarity in the matter when he writes that there are contained in the Catholic doctrine of the *analogia entis* the possibilities of a true incarnational cosmos, including body and soul, community and individual, because in their totality.... they are "open" to God. From the standpoint of the Catholic doctrine of the *analogia entis* creation in its totality is the vision, mounting from likeness to likeness, of the God who is beyond every likeness. It is, therefore, a receptive readiness for Him. In its final essence it is, as it were, already Mary's "Behold, the handmaid of the Lord. Be it unto me according to Thy word" (*Religionsphil. Kath. Theol.* 1926, p. 53).

Aquinas, who thinks that theology studies God the Holy Trinity and can make use of philosophy as a subordinate science in the service of theology.[25] Many Reformed theologians, especially in the Protestant scholastic traditions, have a similar view, and arguably there is a good bit of harmony here between Aquinas and Calvin himself.

However, this now all seems to be obscured. What the Reformation is about, we are told after the Barth–Przywara debate, is a new Barthian idea of unilateral divine activity without human agency, allied with an idea about the absence of any natural knowledge of God in the human community. Now we can only gain access to the classical Reformation "solas" if we also acknowledge these new Barthian truths. Is this correct, however, simply as a reading of the Protestant tradition? It is powerful and intriguing, surely, but I think it falls into the same category within the Protestant community that Przywara's thought falls into within the Catholic community. That is to say, it is an eccentric and deeply original proposition, with the difference that it has been far more influential among Protestants than Przywara's idea has been among Catholics. And with one more very important difference: the methodological extensiveness of Barth's proposal. Effectively, what Barth proposed in *CD* I/1 is related methodologically to the Christological ontology of election, covenant, and creation that he develops later in *CD* II/2 (*Doctrine of the Word of God*, part 2), III/1–2 (*Doctrine of Creation*, parts 1–2), 1–2, and IV/1–2 (*Doctrine of Reconciliation*, parts 1–2). Here he does assimilate and reformulate all kinds of philosophical notions from modernity in

---

25. *ST* I, q. 1, a. 5, ad 2:

This science can in a sense depend upon the philosophical sciences, not as though it stood in need of them, but only in order to make its teaching clearer. *For it accepts its principles not from other sciences, but immediately from God, by revelation.* Therefore it does not depend upon other sciences as upon the higher, but makes use of them as of the lesser, and as handmaidens: even so the master sciences make use of the sciences that supply their materials, as political of military science. That it thus uses them is not due to its own defect or insufficiency, but to the defect of our intelligence, which is more easily led by what is known through natural reason (from which proceed the other sciences) to that which is above reason, such as are the teachings of this science (emphasis mine).

a creative and innovative way—ideas from Hegel, Kant, Sartre and others. So one could believe that those constructive proposals are all somehow logically dependent upon or conceptually intimately related to the ideas of the start, regarding "natural theology" and the conditions of theology. This means that if one is committed to ideas from Barth's later Christology, one is also likely to see them as somehow connected to his earlier ideas of revelation.

Perhaps within the logic of Barth's overall *oeuvre* such connections are indeed essential and must be maintained to make use of any of his later ideas, but this does not seem to be the case, at least in theory. In fact it is fairly simple to articulate an argument to the contrary. Take Barth's theology of the relation of the divine and human essences of Christ in *CD* IV/2, which posits a relational account of the divinity and humanity of Jesus within a dynamic view of the unfolding of the covenant in time as a place where God's Trinitarian pre-history, or eternal identity, is manifest to us precisely in God's Filial human life. It would be possible to develop a more ontologically rich account of these very ideas in conversation with the classical Chalcedonian tradition (Barth in conversation with Maximus the Confessor and Aquinas, for instance) and to make use of concepts developed on "Christian philosophical soil" to do so. This could be done in conversation with Hegelian notions of relation and divine-event ontology and Kantian ideas about the limitations of human knowledge as a moment of explication of the "novelty" of revelation in Christ. But the articulation of all these ideas, to be done properly, would need to include an overt set of reflections about the philosophical warrant of ideas of Maximus, Aquinas, Kant, Hegel, and so forth, and this "moment of philosophical reflection" is lacking in Barth by design. This does not help his case in the end, it seems to me, but rather weakens it considerably, because his notions of topics like "relation" and "event" in God appear overtly incoherent and under-examined. Whether or not I am right about this, I do not think my judgment should be considered "Church dividing," and when the topic is examined historically it seems like a very serious error for a Protestant theologian to think that it is. There are many Lutheran, Reformed, and Anglican theologians who would agree with me and other Catholics on the inevitable uses of philosophy within *sacra doctrina*, as they themselves accept that there is a place for overt philosophical reflection within Christian theology.

The person who saw things similarly and who sought to put the debate in the right framework was Gottlieb Söhngen.[26] Söhngen's essays on the controversy famously influenced Barth, who indicated in a somewhat nebulous way that, if Söhngen's view of the *analogia entis* was correct, he had no difficulty with the doctrine.[27]

Some take Söhngen's view to be a kind of Catholic reformulation of the idea of natural knowledge of God made in concession to Barth's theology, one that anticipates the later theories of Vatican I offered by von Balthasar in his book on Barth. However, Söhngen is well versed in modern scholastic theology and his analysis of the debate is based, as I see it, on the kinds of points I have been making above. Catholic theology studies the object of revelation, God himself, and in doing so, seeks to understand the *analogia fidei* as understood in Catholic thought, which is the likeness or resemblance found between the mysteries, the *nexus mysteriorum*.[28] It can do so by making use of philosophical knowledge of God or creatures, now placed in subordinate service to theological reflection. The latter process presupposes that the philosophical ideas of human culture, including evolving Christian intellectual culture, be analyzed and reformulated in light of divine revelation and ultimately in view of a Christological center of theological reflection on Scripture. The Church's Tradition and way of reading Scripture provide

---

26. See Gottlieb Söhngen, "The Analogy of Faith: Likeness to God from Faith Alone?," trans. K. Oakes, *Pro Ecclesia* 21 (2012): 56–76, and "The Analogy of Faith: Unity in the Science of Faith," trans. K. Oakes, *Pro Ecclesia* 21 (2012): 169–94. The originals appeared in the German theology journal *Catholica* in 1934. However one interprets Barth's claims that he had buried the debate, I agree with Keith Johnson that he in fact held out against natural theology for the duration of his theological career.

27. See the analysis of von Balthasar, *Theology of Karl Barth*, 328–34.

28. See chapter 1 on Söhngen and chapter 2 on the *nexus mysteriorum*.

normative points of reference for the understanding of Scripture as a
unified text and as a text understood in a unified coherent way down
through time (in Church doctrine). Söhngen, in light of this vision,
was critical of the Przywarian definition of theology, which gave a
kind of primacy to philosophical metaphysics, and von Balthasar followed Söhngen on this point, even while insisting against Barth on
the necessity of philosophical metaphysics within Catholic theology. Joseph Ratzinger, the most famous doctoral student of Söhngen,
likewise advanced a very similar vision of the object of theological
science as it relates to philosophical metaphysics.[29]

In the first section of this reflection I have argued that a Thomistic understanding of *sacra doctrina* rightly understood has a place for
contributions from philosophical metaphysics, critically assimilated
in light of divine revelation.

In this second part I have argued that this conception of the use
of philosophy within *sacra doctrina* is not Church dividing. Przywara
and Barth together have bequeathed us a legacy of thinking that it is
or must be. However, I think that this legacy is something of a poi-
soned chalice, one that Protestants and Catholics together should re-
fuse to drink from. The terms of agreement and disagreement should
be re-evaluated, including in Christological conversation. *Ecclesia
semper reformanda est.* Surely if Barthians hold that conciliar definitions such as those of Nicaea and Chalcedon are reformable in principle, they must consider Barth's own "dogmatics of the Church" as
reformable in principle as well (unless Barth has become a paper
pope, on the so-called *analogia entis*). Of course I am not suggesting
that Catholics and Protestants have no significant theological divi-

29. See von Balthasar's criticism of Przywara on this point in *Theo-Logic: Theological
Logical Theory*, vol. 2, *The Truth of God*, trans. A. Walker (San Francisco: Ignatius Press,
2004), 94n16, and the logically congruent remarks on 273n109. For Ratzinger, see *Introduction to Christianity*, trans. J. R. Foster (San Francisco: Ignatius Press, 2000), 74–79,
137–61, and "*In the Beginning...*": *A Catholic Understanding of the Story of Creation and the
Fall*, trans. B. Ramsey (Grand Rapids, MI: Eerdmans, 1998); Pope Benedict XVI, Encyclical Letter *Deus caritas est* (2005), §§10 and 13.

sions among them but only that these need not and should not be framed in terms of the *analogia entis*. Catholics and Protestants can and should argue about the truth or falsehood of diverse Christological ontologies and about the value of various philosophical ontologies, whether classical or modern, but *those* arguments need not be Church-dividing. Referring back to my hierarchical degrees from the first section of the chapter: one can agree on Chalcedonian principles in Christology while belonging to distinct schools of thought that in turn harness concepts from diverse philosophical traditions. There are arguments worth having between the schools, but they are not arguments about the truth of the common creedal confession of faith *per se*.

CONSIDERATION OF A TEST CASE: CHRISTOLOGY AND KENOSIS

Having made these comments about revelation, dogma, schools of theology, philosophy within theology, and the necessary distinctions between them, I would like to consider an example: the idea central to the thought of many modern Catholic and Protestant theologians that the Holy Trinity is revealed especially in the abandonment of Jesus crucified, in his dereliction and suffering unto death. Such an idea is based essentially on the idea of God's solidarity with humanity in our 'godforsakenness,' wherein God has descended by self-emptying (kenosis) into our worst condition of suffering so as to reveal to us what is most ultimate and salvific in God (his life as the Holy Trinity, able to unite us to himself by grace and glory). Let me begin with a stipulation, and then I will make three basic claims.

The stipulation is the following: It is natural to think that the profound existential confusion and moral evil experienced by many in the twentieth century should be the occasion for the Church to meditate theologically upon the crucifixion of God so as to make progress in understanding the mystery of the Trinity revealed by the Cross. My own limited reflection on the cry of dereliction seeks in its own way to acknowledge this facet of modern theology, albeit in a Thomistic light,[30] and I take it that my own analysis bears some resemblance to (and takes inspiration from) that of Pope John Paul II, as attested in a well-known passage in *Novo millennio ineunte*.[31] This view seems close to that of other influential twentieth-century Thomists, such as Charles Journet.[32] These authors, while deeply influenced by Aquinas, were also deeply affected by and engaged with the terrific suffering of human beings evidenced in the mid-twentieth century.

This being said, history is not destiny in theology. Barth proved that in the face of Schleiermacher and Harnack. After their work seemed to have defined modern Protestant academic theology, his work and vision of Protestant theology, at least for a time, displaced theirs. Why then might we prefer modern theologians engaged with the problem of suffering to those who came before? After all, the reflections on the dereliction of Christ crucified found in Catherine of Siena, Thomas Aquinas, Francis of Assisi, Bonaventure, Julian of Norwich, John of the Cross, and Teresa of Ávila should matter to us as much as those found in von Balthasar or Adrienne von Speyr, and

---

30. See White, *The Incarnate Lord*, ch. 7.

31. John Paul II, Apostolic Letter *Novo millennio ineunte* (2001), §26:

> Jesus' cry on the Cross, dear Brothers and Sisters, is not the cry of anguish of a man without hope, but the prayer of the Son who offers his life to the Father in love, for the salvation of all. At the very moment when he identifies with our sin, "abandoned" by the Father, he "abandons" himself into the hands of the Father. His eyes remain fixed on the Father. Precisely because of the knowledge and experience of the Father which he alone has, even at this moment of darkness he sees clearly the gravity of sin and suffers because of it. He alone, who sees the Father and rejoices fully in him, can understand completely what it means to resist the Father's love by sin. More than an experience of physical pain, his Passion is an agonizing suffering of the soul. Theological tradition has not failed to ask how Jesus could possibly experience at one and the same time his profound unity with the Father, by its very nature a source of joy and happiness, and an agony that goes all the way to his final cry of abandonment. The simultaneous presence of these two seemingly irreconcilable aspects is rooted in the fathomless depths of the hypostatic union.

This passage bears remarkable similarities to Aquinas's analysis in *ST* III, q. 46, aa. 6–8.

32. See, for example, Charles Journet, *Les Septs Paroles du Christ au Croix* (Paris: Editions du Seuil, 1954), 88–90.

the views of these former thinkers differ notably from the latter (and sometimes from one another). If the dereliction theology of Barth, von Balthasar, and/or von Speyr is set up as a unique guiding canon to the whole tradition, one may wonder rightly about the method and criteria at work. I do not think the use of this kenotic ontology in von Balthasar comes primarily either from mystical experience or from an insight related to the Barth's rejection of natural theology. It comes, rather, from another source. I am referring here to the important influence upon Barth and von Balthasar of Hegel's Christology, both of whom engaged for and against his positions in diverse ways.

Hegel's Christology and the Ontology of Freedom

Why focus on Hegel in this context? Surely Hegel is one of the most under-examined theologians in modern theological studies, even among those who are most influenced by him. This influence is indirect, mediated through the post-Hegelian Trinitarian theologies of the twentieth century.[33] This is true above all when one thinks of his proposals regarding kenosis in God that stem in great part from his theological innovation with regard to the communication of idioms. Hegel knew of the seventeenth-century debate between the Giessen and Tübingen schools of thought regarding the communication of idioms, the predication of the attributes of the divine and human natures to the person of Christ. Both schools presuppose some version of the *genus majestaticum:* the idea that certain properties of the divine nature may be attributed to the human nature of Christ.[34] In the *Lectures on the Philosophy of Religion*, Hegel inverts

33. See the pertinent analysis of Bruce D. Marshall, "The Absolute and the Trinity," *Pro Ecclesia* 13, no. 2 (2014): 147–64.

34. The former school held that the Son of God made man simply concealed his divine prerogatives during the course of his earthly life, while the other held that he in some sense suspended their use by way of a kenotic self-abandonment of divine properties. Like Aquinas and Calvin, I take it that the very idea of an attribution of the divine attributes (like omnipresence) to the human nature is itself problematic and contrary to the mainstream use of the communication of idioms in patristic representatives such as Gregory of Nazianzus, Cyril of Alexandria, Leo the Great, and John Damascene. They attribute natural properties of each nature not to the alternative nature but only to the person of the Son, who genuinely subsists in each nature, such that the natures are united but not confused.

the perspective of the Tübingen school regarding the *genus majestaticum*. Whereas they speculated on how or in what way the attributes of the deity might be communicated to the humanity, Hegel speculates on how the attributes of the humanity might be communicated to the divinity, a view later referred to as the *genus tapeinoticum*. In virtue of the Incarnation, God is able to take attributes of human finitude, such as temporality, suffering, and death, into his own divine life and being. The foundation for this capacity of the deity is located in God's freedom, his capacity to identify even with his ontological contrary by way of self-exploratory diremption.[35]

Barth rightly identified problems with this view in *CD* IV/1, §59, but he sought to reformulate the idea in what he acknowledged in turn to be a very novel way.[36] The condition of possibility of God taking on human attributes into his own life and essence as God is not grounded in a developmental history of God in the economy (as it is in Hegel) but grounded in an eternal pre-condition in the life of the Trinity, in which the eternal kenotic life of the Son from the Father anticipates (by analogy we could say) the temporal historical life of the Son as human.[37] Von Balthasar in turn adopts this view from Barth, and qualifies it with additional notions from Bulgakov

35. For a characteristic example, see "The Consummate Religion," in Hegel, *Lectures on the Philosophy of Religion, One-Volume Edition: The Lectures of 1827*, trans. R. F. Brown, P. C. Hodgson, J. M. Stewart (Oxford: Clarendon Press, 2006), 452–69, at 468–69:

> "God himself is dead," it says in a Lutheran hymn, expressing an awareness that the human, the finite, the fragile, the weak, the negative are themselves a moment of the divine, that they are within God himself, that finitude, negativity, otherness are not outside of God and do not, as otherness, hinder unity with God. Otherness, the negative, is known to be a moment of the divine nature itself. This involves the highest idea of spirit.... This is the explication of reconciliation: that God is reconciled with the world, that even the human is not something alien to him, but rather that this otherness, this self-distinguishing [of the divine nature through diremption], finitude as it is expressed, is a moment in God himself.

On historical aspects of the communication of idioms in the Tübingen school, see also Walter Kasper, *The Absolute in History: The Philosophy and Theology of History in Schelling's Late Philosophy*, trans. K. Wolff (New York: Paulist Press, 2018), 459–65.

36. See Barth, *CD* IV/1 (London: T&T Clark, 1961), 157–357.

37. See for example Barth, *CD* IV/1, 129, 177, 179.

(who was himself also deeply dependent upon Hegel's conception through the mediation of Thomasius).[38]

Von Balthasar rightly saw that, if this account is to be defended, it requires an exploration of the "similitude" or analogy between the Son as God and the Son in his human dereliction, a similitude cast conceptually in ways that are not previously anticipated in the classical Christian tradition. This is especially the case since, in light of the moves Hegel and Barth make, we now seek to identify the eternal mutual relations of persons in the Trinity through a study of the kenotic human actions and sufferings of Jesus. The Son's obedient self-offering to the Father in the abandonment is the outward economic face of an inward immanent Trinitarian love of mutual freedom, characteristic of the eternal differentiation of the Father and the Son. Freedom of mutually self-giving *wills* (in the plural) seems now to become the key to an understanding of all divine and human ontology.

Thus we are faced with the obligation to undertake a rejection or radically dialectical reassessment of key elements of the patristic and medieval tradition. Most notably, von Balthasar realizes that the psychological analogy for the processions of the Son and Spirit according to a likeness of Word and Love from the Father will have to be abandoned (though it is arguably biblical in origin).[39] Consequently

38. See, in this regard, the important notion of a Trinitarian inversion in von Balthasar, *Theo-Drama: Theological Dramatic Theory*, vol. 3, *The Dramatis Personae: Persons in Christ*, trans. G. Harrison (San Francisco: Ignatius Press, 1993), 183–91 and 521–23. The processions of the Son and the Spirit are supposedly inverted in the economy: due to the kenosis of the Son, during the time of his Incarnation and prior to the resurrection, the Son proceeds from the Spirit and is utterly relative to him not merely in his human instincts of mind and heart (i.e., in virtue of Christ's capital grace) but rather in his very person and being as Son. Likewise consider the thematic argument of Bulgakov, *The Lamb of God*, trans. B. Jakim (Grand Rapids, MI: Eerdmans, 2008), 247–63, who interprets the Third Council of Constantinople in a kenotic way, so that the human consciousness of Christ in his historical life, suffering, and dereliction is *commensurate* with his divine self-emptying love. The distinction of natures is reinterpreted as a diremption of the divine nature into a human form.

39. See the very clear remarks in *Theo-Logic: Theological Logical Theory*, vol. 2, *Truth of God*, trans. A. Walker, (San Francisco: Ignatius Press, 2004), 128–34, where von Balthasar distances himself from the psychological analogy and then proposes an alternative conception of divine self-emptying love (pp. 134–37).

the central theological motif in all of Western Trinitarian theology is in fact displaced in modern Catholic theology, in light of the novel insights of Hegel and Barth. Traditional theology of the unity of God, based on the study of the shared divine attributes and in particular based on the unity of will in the three persons, is also now rethought in light of an ontology of primal reciprocal freedom.[40]

Of course one can argue that all this represents the right direction for Catholic theology to go in light of the modern insights of Hegel, Bulgakov, and Barth. However, my suspicion is that we should return to Hegel and ask whether he interpreted the communication of idioms correctly and whether Barth and von Balthasar made the right decision to try to develop this new "school" of analogy. Hegel departs in problematic ways from the classical tradition in this domain, and in turn there are problems with the decision to assimilate, reformulate, and "correct" his thought Christologically in the way these later theologians undertake to do. In the final part of my argument I will explain briefly what I take the better option to consist in.

Dyothelitism and the Christological *Analogia Entis*

There is of course a genuine likeness between the human nature and activity of Christ as human and his divine nature and activity as Lord and God. The former is reflective in some way of the latter, even when the Son voluntarily suffers, is crucified, and dies. The dyothelitist principle established by the Third Council of Constantinople,

---

40. See von Balthasar, *Theo-Logic*, 2, 94–95, 173–218, 273n109. Likewise, see *Epilogue*, trans. E. Oakes (San Francisco: Ignatius Press, 2004), 89–90:

> How can Jesus say of himself, "I am the Truth?" This is possible only because all that is true in the world "hold[s] together" in him (Col. 1:17), which in turn presupposes that the *analogia entis* is personified in him, that he is the adequate sign, surrender, and expression of God within finite being. To approach this mystery we must try to think: In God himself the total epiphany, self-surrender, and self-expression of God the Father *is* the Son, identical with him as God, in whom everything—even everything that is possible for God—is expressed. Only if God freely decides in the Son to bring forth a fullness of non-divine beings can the Son's essentially "relative" and thus "kenotic" act in God be seen as a personal act (*esse completum subsistens*) within the act of creation that gives to everything its real identity (*esse completum sed non subsistens*).

following Maximus the Confessor, notes that there is a distinction of two natures in Christ and thus also a distinction of two activities (or natural operations) and wills. However, it is also the case that each "set" of operations is attributed only to one subject and person, the eternal person of the Son, who is truly divine and acts as Lord and truly human and acts and suffers as man.[41] The human actions and sufferings are therefore also (1) subordinate to the divine actions and (2) expressive of the Son's personal identity and nature as God. In short, all that Jesus does and suffers in his human nature, life, and operations is indicative of his divine Sonship and at least obliquely indicative of the divine work he is accomplishing with the Father and the Holy Spirit.

It follows from this that the mode in which Jesus is human (his distinctive way of subsisting uniquely in human nature) is utterly personal and filial, due to the hypostatic union. His nature, grace, actions, and sufferings *as human* are always *revelatory* of his personal being as Son, who exists in personal filial relation to the Father and to the Spirit (in distinct ways) in all that he is and does. To illustrate this idea, we might consider Jesus's highest form of human knowledge: is Jesus's beatific or immediate vision as man (by which he knows the Father immediately and intuitively in the heights of his human intellect by grace) specifically the same as ours or is it filial in mode, in a way that is distinct from the beatification of other human beings? Theologically, we must say that this is a false disjunctive and that both ideas are to be affirmed. The beatific vision of Christ in his earthly life pertains to him as man, and thus is distinctly human in species, but it is also the vision of the Son, and so it is distinctly filial in mode, and proper in this respect to the Son made man. If Jesus's beatific vision is not specifically of the same kind as ours, then God has not truly identified himself with us in our condition as human and has not truly realized our salvation as one of us from within our human condition. Here the famous claim of Gregory of

41. I have tried to give greater articulation to this idea in "Dyotheletism and the Consciousness of Christ," *Pro Ecclesia* 17 (2008): 396–422.

Nazianzus to Apollinarius applies: what God has not assumed he has not saved. However, if Jesus has this immediate vision as a human being, he also has it in a filial way, as the Son made man, much as he is humanly free but also acts freely as the Son of God, always from and in relation to his Father and in conformity with his own divine willing. When the Son is humanly conscious of God, he is humanly conscious of the Father being his Father, and of being the Son of the Father, and of being the co-principle of the Father's Spirit, whom he wishes to send upon the world.[42]

We may recognize, then, a two-fold truth in this regard. The human nature of God the Son does truly reveal his divine identity and the relations of the Father, Son, and Holy Spirit, as these relations are manifest in Jesus's human life, suffering, death, and exaltation. However, this revelation of the filial identity of the Son in his earthly life can only take place because the human nature and actions of Jesus possess a distinctively filial mode of expression proper to the Son made man.

To recognize all this, however, is to acknowledge also the difference of the human nature qua nature from the divine, as it is truly man that God has become, and indeed God has become human precisely to express his inner mystery of Sonship in flesh and blood within our human sphere. This presupposes the difference and analogical dissimilitude of the two natures, not only the likeness. There is no strict identity between the humanity of God and his divinity, nor can there be.

However, it is just this real distinction of natures that is compromised by Hegel's innovative use of the communication of idioms, since he transmits the human attributes into God and evacuates the divine attributes, or at least makes them disposable at the discretion of God's evolving freedom in history. Barth does something very different but arguably more radical, since he renders the human attri-

---

42. John 15:26: "But when the Counselor comes, whom I shall send to you from the Father, even the Spirit of truth, who proceeds from the Father, he will bear witness to me."

butes "always, already" present in God as the condition of possibility for the personal differentiation of the Father and the Son.[43] In various ways, Pannenberg, von Balthasar, Jüngel, and Moltmann are all downstream from this decision, and they commonly adopt this way of proceeding, albeit in various ways and with significant and interesting differences between them.

What emerges in all these thinkers, due to this primal conceptual decision, is what may be termed a form of "inverted monophysitism," in which the divine nature of the Son is conceived of not in terms of analogical similitude but in fact by way of univocity. Simply put, the properties and characteristics of the human nature of Jesus, particularly in his voluntary acts of freedom, obedience, suffering, dereliction, experience of abandonment as separation, and death, are transposed onto the divine nature, as indicative of a polarity in God that exists between the Father and the Son eternally. I do not think this inverted monophysitism comes from a close reading of St. Paul but from the Christology of Hegel, and I take it that this is a matter of historical fact, not speculation, and one that can be verified readily not by an attentive historical study of the New Testament but by a close historical-critical study of Barth and von Balthasar in their proximate intellectual context.[44]

I am in no way denying that these thinkers aspire to read Scripture in harmony with the Chalcedonian tradition, and I am not claiming that they are necessarily less orthodox or more philosoph-

43. I argue this at further length in "Crucified Lord."
44. In passing I should note that my concern is that modern kenotic theology in practice if not always in theory risks collapsing the distinction of natures, characterizing the divine nature of the Son by reference to his human mode of being, thus projecting irreducibly and uniquely human traits onto the transcendent divine nature. It is worth noting that this theological tendency can have very detrimental effects on the Church's theological conversation with adherents of modern Judaism and Islam, who would tend to see in this kind of inverted monophysitism the danger of a projection in Christianity of human attributes onto the divine nature that obscures one's rightful acknowledgment of the transcendence of the divinity of God. This is not to say that I advocate for any form of Nestorianism, classical or revised. John Damascene's Chalcedonianism is a model in this respect for dialogue between Western and Eastern Christians and for conversation with Jews and Muslims regarding the transcendence of God.

ical that Aquinas. They take up other options as theologians, making proximate use of philosophical ideas critically, and therefore simply present us with a distinctive school of thought, or perhaps two schools of thought. What I am claiming, however, is that what their schools argue on this point is in fact disadvantageous to a better understanding of Scripture regarding the kenotic suffering of Christ as indicative of the inner reality of the Trinity (which it is in some way).

This argument allows one to return to the question of a need for analogical reflection in both Chalcedonian Christology and metaphysics as distinct but interrelated modes of reflection. Von Balthasar certainly does aspire, with sophistication, to distinct and related forms of reflection on such topics, and he wanted as well to speak about the *analogia entis Christi*.[45] However when he speaks of the eternal Son under the auspices of human actions and sufferings, I take it that he is in fact speaking univocally of the divine nature in human terms. This kind of discourse could be metaphorical at best, but of course followers of von Balthasar do not interpret him in this way, nor should they, if they wish to present accurately von Balthasar's own (to my mind implausible, problematic) claims. If the Triune God is incomprehensibly but truly one in being and one in will, as the Church basing herself on Scripture teaches is the case, then there is no eternal obedience, surrender, infinite distance, separation, self-emptying, or suffering in God. To the extent that we use these notions to describe the inner life of the Trinity, I think we step out of the world of the Bible and into a new form of univocity theory, in which all-too-human attributes are hypostatized. Instead we should return to the use of the psychological analogy and the theology of divine attributes as a way to understand the eternal processions of the Word and Spirit, who each possess in themselves eternally from the Father the undiminishable plenitude of divine life. The Tradition provides us already with this distinctive theological analogy

---

45. It is interesting to notice how with this term from von Balthasar we are somehow back to Przywara's non-philosophical usage of the notion of the *analogia entis*, but now from the top down, as it were, knowing all being in light of the mystery of Christ.

of what is proper to the inner life of the Trinity: the Son is the eternal Logos of the Father, and the Spirit is the eternal Love of the Father and the Son. However, in *sacra doctrina* as I understand it, we can press forward with this analogy of the immanent eternal life of the Trinity to ask more overtly the question that the post-Hegelian theologians ask. How does the mystery of the Cross reveal God, the Holy Trinity? Might we offer new answers to this question, other than those presented by von Balthasar, even if we also remain in dialogue with his great work?

What then would be the way forward in a deeper dialogue between Thomists and Balthasarians? We would need to think about Christological principles and how we each hold to them, especially in the interpretation of the communication of idioms and the teaching of the Third Council of Constantinople regarding dyothelitism, and we would *also* need to talk about analogical terms for the divine nature and what should and can, or should not and cannot be predicated of the eternal nature and life of the one God.

I take it that many ideas of Barth in *CD* II/1 regarding attributes of the one God could be of help in this conversation. Many modern post-Hegelian theologians, Catholic as well as Protestant, fail to engage in any sustained way with the tradition of the divine attributes of the one God received from the classical theological tradition, both patristic and medieval. What ought we to make today of the divine simplicity, goodness, unity, omnipotence, infinity, and so on? In that volume Barth engages in profound conversation with figures like Augustine, Boethius, and Aquinas in considering the Church's confession *de Deo ut uno*: on God as essentially one, in his freedom, eternity, sovereignty, universal presence, and other attributes. This reflection has a grounding in the classical tradition even as it engages with modern questions in a creative way. As such it can contribute to an ongoing discussion of the Church's common confession of the *unity* of the Triune God and the *real distinction* of the divine and human natures of the incarnate Lord. In pursuing such topics together, Protestant and Catholic theologians alike can contribute in fraternal collaboration to the responsibilities and work of Christology. This example is interesting because it suggests that sometimes Catholics can also allow themselves to be inspired or provoked by Protestant theologians so as to recover profound elements of their own tradition and in doing so to rethink their content and expression in a contemporary setting. This kind of ecumenical practice can also invite non-Catholic Christians to consider anew the depths and specific doctrinal and philosophical content of the Catholic tradition, as well as to think with and for Catholics about how the classical truths of conciliar theology may be proclaimed today with renewed understanding and vigor.

4

Thomism after Vatican II

INTRODUCTION: THOMISTIC PRINCIPLES AND
DIALOGICAL ENGAGEMENT IN MODERNITY

By the end of the Second Vatican Council, it had become custom-
ary for many attending the event itself to speak of the "minority"
party and the "majority." This terminology is employed unselfcon-
sciously, for example, in the journal of Yves Congar as he writes in
1964 and 1965.[1] Both parties were quite possibly in fact mere numer-
ic minorities within a larger whole, but they represented ideological
tendencies vying for influence. In retrospect, we can say that they
were divided by a common question: how should the Church understand herself and her mission in the modern world in the wake
of the decline of ancient monarchical regimes and the rise of modern secular democracies? Both sides were, in a certain sense, seeking to preserve the fullness of Catholic teaching and to promote
that teaching in the modern era.

Both hoped for the reunion of the Church with the predominant culture but with differing points of emphasis. One tendency
was to see this aim in primarily conservationalist terms, the minority
emphasizing the preservation of authentic intellectual and spiritual

1. Yves Congar, *My Journal of the Council*, trans. M. J. Ronayne and M. C. Boulding,
ed. D. Minns (Collegeville, MN: Liturgical Press, 2012). The terms are commonly employed throughout these years of notes.

traditions, over against an increasingly non-religious modern secularism. The other tendency, the seeming majority, was to see this aim in dialogical or primarily optimistic terms, aiming for a kind of renovation, and seeking opportunities in the signs of the times for a way to bring the Church's message to modern man.

Neither side in this engagement wanted to do away with the privileged study of Thomas Aquinas in the life of the Church, but they tended to envisage that study in fairly different terms. Here one might consider two of the most balanced voices, one from either side. First, then, consider Cornelius Fabro. The renowned Italian Thomistic scholar, an Angelicum graduate, was asked to compose a *votum* in the early 1960s as part of the commission on seminary education that would eventually produce *Optatam Totius*.[2] Fabro predicted that in the coming years after the Council there would continue to develop in European civilization a postreligious subjectivism that he denoted by the classical antimodernist term "immanentism."[3] He foretold that this cultural tendency would lead to a two-fold error: on the one hand, an extreme form of skeptical rationalism that takes any appeal to transcendent metaphysical truths about God, or teachings of divine revelation, to be unwarranted impositions of past authorities upon the contemporary freedom of human consciousness to derive for itself the content of personal truth claims (in effect the rise of extreme versions of private truth theories). On the other hand, there would be what he termed an extreme fideism: a theology that takes refuge in the integrity of traditional forms of thought without due reference to metaphysical realism, the philosophical study of nature, ethical objectivity, or a healthy con-

2. Cornelio Fabro, "De Doctrina S. Thomae in Scholis Catholicis Promovenda," *Acta et Documenta* IV/II/1 (Typis Polyglottis Vaticanis, 1961), 177–89. See the commentary by Joseph A. Komonchak, "Thomism and the Second Vatican Council," in *Continuity and Plurality in Catholic Theology: Essays in Honor of Gerald A. McCool, S. J.*, ed. A. J. Cemera (Fairfield, CT: Sacred Heart University Press, 1998), 53–73.

3. "Immanentism" is a larger analytic theme in Fabro's work that he treats with insight. See *God in Exile: Modern Atheism. A Study of the Internal Dynamic of Modern Atheism, from Its Roots in the Cartesian Cogito to the Present Day*, trans. A. Gibson (New York: Newman, 1968; Italian ed. 1964), esp. 1061–1153.

fidence in the positive relation between supernatural faith and the natural sciences. To remedy this two-fold tendency of subjectivism and fideism, which Fabro predicts will enter deeply into the life of future clergy as well as Catholic laity, he counsels a sophisticated engagement with the study of St. Thomas in both seminaries and Catholic universities. Here he notes the importance of the consideration of the first principles of speculative and practical reason, study of metaphysics and of the constitution of the human person in Thomistic terms (hylomorphic personalism), knowledge of the arguments for the existence of God, consideration of the relation of creation to the modern natural sciences, and so forth.

Second, consider Yves Congar. Interestingly, Congar saw the Council as a kind of vindication of Thomism, at least in its spirit or method of procedure. (Note that this is quite different from Joseph Ratzinger, who thought the event signaled a new paradigmatic shift in theology toward the *ressourcement* of older patristic models of engagement with culture, rather than those represented by scholasticism.) In an essay published in 1967 Congar contrasted two visions of Thomism at the Council, one particularly focused upon "a system of abstractions and of prefabricated solutions" to intellectual problems.[4] He associates this form of Thomism with the early modern French Dominican, Charles René Billuart, as a paradigmatic example. He claims that it developed out of the longstanding rivalries between religious orders and their theological schools (Thomism versus Scotism, Suarezianism, etc), and that it is more animated by interecclesial quarrels seeking to define theology from within than by genuine engagement in cultural evangelization of the living world around the Church.[5] Catholic intellectual life is most healthy, by contrast, when it engages with the real intellectual puzzles of its age and helps to make the Gospel most accessible to those both inside and outside the Church by resolving the questions of the day

4. Yves Congar, "La Théologie au Concile. Le « théologiser » du Concile," *in Situation et Taches Présentes de la Théologie* (Paris: Cerf, 1967), 55.
5. Congar, "La Théologie au Concile," 54.

in the light of Christ. In other words, Catholic theology should be missionary in nature. Congar claims that the Council follows the example of Aquinas in this regard: "Saint Thomas was not a man who repeated categories and conclusions supposedly formulated once and for all. He spent his life seeking out new texts, in overseeing the production of new translations ... in dialogue with all the 'heretics' of his time, those who did not think like him, either within or outside of the Church." "The Council is right," Congar adds, "we should not repeat his theses but rather place ourselves in his school of thought."[6]

The implication seems to be that we should do today what Aquinas did in his own age, by engaging with the thought-world and questions of our era. Congar then gives a succinct list of the main theological issues of the day, as he sees them in 1967. What does his list consist in? How theology might engage with modern exegesis, the tasks of ecumenism with the Orthodox and the Reformed, questions posed by Marxism, the Church's response to modern psychology, the sexual revolution and the newly developed contraceptive pill, and the atomic bomb and the threat of mass extinction through means of modern warfare.[7] The list is not synonymous with the concerns of our epoch over 50 years later; nor is it entirely alien either.

Nothing transpired after the Council precisely as anyone had expected it to, and great changes occurred. To give but a partial list: there were the student revolutions of 1968 only a few years later, the sexual revolution had consequences no one predicted (still unfolding in dramatic ways), a steep decline of religious practice took place in Europe and North America (now continuing in South America), the expansion of Catholicism grew vibrantly in the southern hemisphere in Africa and Asia, Marxism fell and gave way to a new internationalist market economy animated by new forms of technology, secular liberalism and capitalism became ascendant, the postmodern critique of philosophical modernity dissolved many of the common

6. Congar, "La Théologie au Concile," 55.
7. Congar, "La Théologie au Concile," 56.

philosophical presuppositions of the twentieth century European universities, and computer technology altered world communication and the economy irreversibly. And also, the pontificate of John Paul II took place, which offered an intellectually plausible and spiritually profound vision of Catholicism in the midst of the modern world over a period of twenty-seven years, which I would argue continues to play out as the normative influence in the Church's intellectual engagement with modernity and her interpretation of the Second Vatican Council.[8]

Without seeking to evaluate here the many facets of the Council and its aftermath, I would simply like to state at this juncture that I take Fabro and Congar to both be correct but each in a different respect. For one, Thomism is above all an integral way of seeing the world, rightly, in light of realistic principles. It is a *scientia* and a *sapientia*: an explanatory science and a form of wisdom. For the other, it represents an intellectual stance of the Catholic intellectual life: a vitality of engagement with the contemporary issues of one's age, in the service of evangelization. So, following both Fabro and Congar, we may speak of two poles of emphasis: integrity of principles, vitality of engagement. Evidently, no opposition between these two is required, but there is a need to understand them in a proper order. Toward that end, we can reflect briefly on each point, with a view toward answering the question posed implicitly by the title of this chapter: what should Thomism after Vatican II aspire to do?

THE INTEGRITY OF THOMISM: PRINCIPLES
AND INWARD CONSTITUTION

Toward the first point, then, let us consider the integrity of Thomism. What is it essentially? First we may note that it is unhelpful and im-

8. See in this respect the insightful analysis of George Weigel in "Rescuing *Gaudium et Spes*: The New Humanism of John Paul II," *Nova et Vetera* (English edition) 8 (2010): 251–67. Weigel emphasizes the continuity between the pontificate of John Paul II and the aspirations of *Gaudium et spes*, but he also shows how those aspirations had to be translated into a very different context than that anticipated by the Council Fathers.

plausibly minimalistic to define Thomism in merely meta-historical methodological terms. This is what one does when one affirms that "Thomism" represents merely the valid aspiration to do in our own time what Aquinas did in his: to create a unique Christian vision by dialectic out of the myriad incompatible web of opinions that currently occupies our own cultural intellectual space. That might be an aspiration inspired by the example of Aquinas, or not, but certainly it is not a stable or integral form of thought. It is nothing like the "perennial philosophy" that is alluded to in recent ecclesial documents like *Optatam totius*, *Fides et ratio*, and *Veritatis gaudium*, each of which advocate explicitly for the study and transmission of the philosophical and theological patrimony of Thomas Aquinas.[9]

On the other extreme, it seems like it is a danger to define Thomism merely by reference to Aquinas's most unique philosophical and theological theses, those teachings which set him apart even in the thirteenth century from his scholastic contemporaries. I am alluding to theses like those of the real distinction between *esse* and essence in all created beings (dear to Étienne Gilson as the chief moniker of Aquinas's thought), his particular doctrine of participation, his affirmation of the soul as the subsistent form of the body, such that the person is one composite substance composed of body and soul, and his teaching on the agent intellect as the natural principle of human cognition.[10] Or in theology: his treatment of the persons of the Trinity as subsistent relations, his doctrine of infused moral virtues, the theology of transubstantiation, his particular theory of the character of priestly ordination, and so forth. Surely these insights are part of the Thomistic heritage, but taken in themselves, they would represent too narrow a definition of his intellectual proj-

---

9. Vatican II. Decree on *Priestly Training Optatam totius* (October 28, 1965), §§15–16; John Paul II, Encyclical Letter *Fides et ratio* (September 14, 1998), §§85 and 87; Francis, Apostolic Constitution Veritatis gaudium (December 8, 2017), §64.1.

10. Étienne Gilson, *L'Être et l'Essence*, 2nd ed. (Paris: J. Vrin, 1972); Cornelio Fabro, *Participation et causalité selon saint Thomas d'Aquin* (Louvain: Publications Universitaires de Louvain, 1961); Joseph Ratzinger, *Eschatology: Death and Eternal Life*, trans. M. Waldstein and A. Nichols (Washington, DC: The Catholic University of America Press, 1988), esp. 178–80. On the unique character of Aquinas's doctrine of the agent intellect, see Fernand Van Steenberghen, *La Philosophie au XIIIe Siècle* (Louvain: Éditions Peeters, 1991).

ect, and a psychologically insecure and excessively negative one: as if we might understand Thomism primarily by understanding how Aquinas's thought is not like anyone else's.

Instead, perhaps we might say the following. First, philosophically speaking, Thomism is, broadly conceived, a Christian Aristotelianism based in the classical philosophical patrimony, expanded organically and developed insightfully in the light of Christian revelation. Thus, the Thomistic heritage typically transmits certain principles that derive originally from Aristotle himself, and that are maintained and promoted not only by Aquinas, but which are common to the broader scholastic community as well. I am thinking here of non-trivial examples like: the epistemological distinction between the speculative and practical intellect, the study of the categorical modes of being and the four causes, the hylomorphic theory of matter and form as the co-constituent principles of nature, the understanding of the soul as the form of a living body, the distinction between substance and accidents, actuality and potency, a teleological theory of human agency, and a virtue-based account of morality. At the same time, Thomism does entail a unique account of this broader philosophical patrimony that is marked radically in its very depths by the Christian tradition and by Aquinas's original genius and insight in interpreting that tradition. Consider in this respect the kinds of doctrines that were mentioned above taken as Thomistic species within a common scholastic genus: St. Thomas's metaphysics of the real distinction as an interpretation of act/potency distinction, his interpretation of the transcendentals, his philosophical treatment of creation, the arguments for the incorruptibility and subsistence after death of the human rational soul (itself the subsistent form of the human body), Aquinas's own very original account of the human emotions, and his theory of various moments of human free action and the treatment of moral objects, ends, and circumstances. We could continue to expand the list. The main point, however, is the following: Thomism *does contain*, philosophically speaking, a coherent body of doctrine, an account of the structure of reality, and

is at the same time well-grounded in the larger tradition of classical European philosophy as well as patristic and medieval theology. It cannot be reduced to a sociological motif or a merely formal
intellectual aspiration, devoid of clear content. To understand what
Aquinas is proposing and arguing for in regard to the nature of reality, one must develop a habit of consideration of reality itself, seeking
to understand if the analysis given by the Thomistic tradition makes
sense, is defensible, and is organically unified or not. The truth about
reality is at stake, not mere procedure. And at the same time, Aquinas's thinking is rooted in a larger tradition of conversation. It does
not emerge ex nihilo as a view from nowhere to be interpreted only
in a hermeneutic of discontinuity with his forebears or successors,
as if to be a Thomist, one had to embrace some stark version of a
Heideggerian metanarrative wherein everyone else has forgotten the
essential, except Aquinas and a few privileged modern interpreters.[11]

Second, theologically speaking, Aquinas's theology takes its
point of departure from the teaching of Christ and the apostles, as
transmitted and understood by the Church. Aquinas as a theologian
is a model in his own right, as he is constantly seeking to understand
the principles of divine revelation, and the order intrinsic to these
principles. His thought is, in this respect, both historical and analytic, biblical and patristic, but also scholastic, rational, and demonstrative ... and at times also intuitive and mystical. Reading Aquinas teaches one how to think theologically. To say that Aquinas is a
great theologian is not to deny that he is a great philosopher. As he
himself points out, *sacra doctrina* ordinarily makes use of a number

11. I am referring here, for example, to Martin Heidegger's treatment of the history
of metaphysics in his 1929 *The Fundamental Concepts of Metaphysics: World, Finitude, Solitude,* trans. W. McNeill and N. Walker (Bloomington: Indiana University Press, 2001),
41–57, which lays the foundation for what he would subsequently say concerning ontotheology. Authors who follow this line of thought typically seek to "save" Aquinas from
the accusation of ontotheology, against the background of a sea of medieval error. Consider, for example, Jean-Luc Marion, "Saint Thomas d'Aquin et l'onto-théo-logie," *Revue
Thomiste* 95 (1995): 31–66. See the recent criticisms of Heidegger's approach to medieval
philosophy by Jan Aertsen, *Medieval Philosophy as Transcendental Thought: From Philip
the Chancellor to Francesco Suárez* (Leiden: Brill, 2012); esp. 6–7, 631–34, 674–77.

of philosophical, historical, and scientific theories that are not derived immediately from revelation but which enter into the speculative habit of theology, just because theology can and must make use
of them.[12] A clear example would pertain to the humanity of Jesus
Christ. Christian theology acknowledges the truth that God has become human, but it also must ask for this very reason, what does it
mean, philosophically speaking, to be human? Answers to this last
question may contribute constructively to our theological considerations. What should we believe about the body and soul of Christ,
his human intellect and will, the nature of his human death, and resurrection? Here, inevitably, philosophical views impact our particular exposition of the theological mystery. And simultaneously, the
consideration of the mystery of God made possible by the Catholic
theological tradition continually invites every person qua philosopher to adjust or rethink his or her views.

When we speak of a Thomistic theological tradition, then, we
are denoting something complex. Certainly, it is a kind of robust
scholastic theology, one that is historically well-informed and that
is placed at the service of the magisterium. It is affected in distinct
ways by Aquinas's philosophical choices. But it is also characterized
by Aquinas's distinctly theological insights and acumen. Norbert
Del Prado made this argument many years ago in his famous work
on Thomism as a Christian philosophy.[13] He argued there, for example, that Aquinas's metaphysics of the distinction in creatures of
esse and essence and his corresponding doctrine of divine simplicity
contributed in important ways to his articulation of the divine persons of the Trinity as subsistent relations.[14] God is simple, without
composition of *esse* and essence so that he is essentially his own existence, and simultaneously, God the Father, Son, and Holy Spirit
are each the one God, the Creator.[15] Therefore there is nothing that

---

12. *ST* I, q. 1, a. 5, ad 2.

13. Norbert Del Prado, *De veritate fundamentali philosophiae christianae* (Fribourg:
Consociatio Sancti Pauli, 1911), esp. 493–640.

14. Del Prado, *De veritate fundamentali philosophiae christianae*, 516–44.

15. *ST* I, q. 3, aa. 4 and 7; q. 39, aa. 1–2.

distinguishes the persons of the Trinity with respect to essence or existence, and each person must be considered in his subsistence to possess the simple plenitude of the divine being.[16] Consequently, the persons are distinguished only by their relations of origin, which are interpreted in light of the processions of the Son from the Father, and of the Spirit from the Father and the Son. The persons are then "subsistent relations": each one is relative to another in all that he is, and each one contains in himself the perfection and plenitude of the divine essence, the Father giving the Son to be, by way of generation, the Father and the Son giving the Spirit to be, by way of spiration.[17] In his notion of the persons as subsistent relations, Aquinas offered the Church, then, a particularly balanced form of Trinitarian monotheism because he managed to acknowledge in a very profound way simultaneously both the absolute primacy of the divine unity and the absolute primacy of the distinction of divine persons. Arguably, this articulation of the mystery of God has not been surpassed by any other exponent of the doctrine.

My point in giving this example is not to claim that Aquinas's theology is special because of his metaphysics. Nor is the point to claim that all Catholic theologians need to be Thomists. To affirm that is to mistake Thomism for the doctrine of the Church, which it clearly is not. Instead, the point is simply to underscore by these limited examples, that Thomism has an essence. It constitutes an identifiable intellectual patrimony that deeply affects the long-term health and stability of the Catholic intellectual heritage in the dual domains of philosophy and theology. If Thomism has a role to play in the age we live in since the Second Vatican Council, this is clearly due to the integrity of the principles of Thomistic thought as a way of thinking about reality.

---

16. Del Prado, *De veritate fundamentali philosophiae christianae*, 530–37.

17. *ST* I, q. 27, aa. 1–2. See the study of this idea by Emmanuel Perrier, *La fécundité en Dieu: La puissance notionnelle dans la Trinité selon saint Thomas d'Aquin* (Paris: Parole et Silence, 2009).

DIALOGUE AND DIALECTIC: ON THE NOTION AND
PRACTICE OF A LIVING THOMISTIC TRADITION

Congar, as I have noted, was concerned after the Second Vatican Council to categorize the contribution of Thomism in terms of dialogue with the thought world of one's age, and I have recast this categorization in terms of "vitality." A living Thomism must not only transmit the integral knowledge of principles but also engage with contemporary issues in the service of evangelization. Here we should be careful: simply being in dialogue should not be confused with authentic vitality. In fact, dialogue is not always the sign of vitality. It is sometimes the sign of decline and capitulation, or mere stagnation. But what Congar was denoting rightly is the following sociological truth: no living spiritual tradition (secular or religious) may win over the culture of its age unless it can address and resolve the key intellectual and ethical problems internal to that culture. This idea applies, of course, not only to the larger cultures outside the ambit of the Catholic Church but also to the culture of the Church. At the time of the Second Vatican Council the Church was faced by a number of important modern theological difficulties that affected the culture of the Church from within and that required some form of address. Whether or not one is satisfied by the solutions to such problems that were offered by the likes of de Lubac and Ratzinger or Rahner and Chenu (whether by *Communio* or *Concilium* schools of thought, for example), it is clear that these movements were attempting to offer solutions to queries of their epoch. It is not sufficient to have the right ideas and to harbor them protectively unless you can also communicate a renewed sense of their vitality and helpfulness in a context in which they are needed. In other words, we stand in need of articulations of Thomism sufficiently concentrated and integral so as to be real and useful, but also accessible, and pertinent, evangelical, and hopeful, so as to be missionary.

We might argue that in the past fifty years it has become painfully apparent that many of the influential theologies of the postconciliar period *are not* today in any position to attempt to replace Thomism from the pre-conciliar period as a normative guide to modern Catholic intellectual life. The theological anthropology of Karl Rahner that greatly influenced the life of the Church in the 1970s presumed a kind of normative modern European intellectual consensus in the academy and the Church that no longer exists today, a Kantian intellectual culture with influences from Hegel and Heidegger.[18] That consensus has perished in the flames of postmodernism, affected also by the rise of analytic philosophy and the return of scientific positivism (influences that do not of course always overlap and that do often conflict with one another). Students in the contemporary university do not suffer from the bias of an intellectually unwarranted pre-commitment to the categories of a stifling pre-modern metaphysics, an unyielding scholastic perennial philosophy repeated without reflection. In fact, they have no access to such a tradition. Rather, they suffer acutely from the lack of any normative philosophical orientation or basic unified intellectual formation at all.[19] Typically they are offered no unifying account of reality that spans across the diversity of their intellectual disciplines. And indeed, where could they procure one? University culture today is characteristically dominated by constructivistic postmodernism, the politics of capitalist liberalism, and scientist positivism (each of which offer very truncated visions of reality, and which are in fact profoundly incompatible with one another). Students often long for some way to make sense of the unity of philosophical experience, so as to see how the world might have some analyzable, overarching meaning. Additionally, if they are Catholic, they wish to see how the various disciplines of learning, whether scientific, philosophical or literary, relate to the theological tenets of their faith. Paradoxically, in this context, the Thomism that was viewed by many as an impasse to the promo-

18. See on this point R. R. Reno, "Rahner the Restorationist: Karl Rahner's Time Has Passed," *First Things* (May 2013).

19. See the diagnosis of Alasdair MacIntyre, *Three Rival Versions of Moral Enquiry* (Notre Dame, IN: University of Notre Dame Press, 1990).

tion of the Church's academic and cultural relevance at the time of the Council increasingly can be understood to be of a unique relevance. However ironic it may seem, the aspirations of a book like Maritain's *Degrees of Knowledge* are of helpful and critical importance in the juncture in which we live today.[20]

Certainly, I am not suggesting that Thomism should be presented under a triumphalistic banner as a potential solution to all contemporary intellectual problems, nor that the famous twenty-four Thomistic theses of the early twentieth century are somehow the appropriate resource that one should turn to so as to respond to questions that arise from the thought of John Rawls, Michel Foucault, or Gianni Vattimo. The claim I am making is more focused. In our own age, Thomism has become one of the only plausible contenders present that provides an authentic vision of the sapiential unity of human knowledge amidst the diversity of university disciplines. Politically, the situation of those who self-identify as Thomists is one of cultural disenfranchisement, to be sure. Those who teach Aquinas are almost complete outsiders in the modern university context, and they can sometimes be characterized as an underground movement who right-thinking people should treat as somehow unwelcome in public discourse. But the rivals who today are offering either within the Church or within the non-religious academic world an alternative account of the intellectual life that is compelling (that is to say, metaphysically non-reductionistic, and epistemically responsible) are few in number and are not having such a tranquil time themselves. As a Dominican friar of the province of Toulouse famously said in the 1970s during an episodic period of particular turmoil: "Brothers, things are bad here, but by the grace of God, they are worse elsewhere." If one's sociological goal is to win the confidence of the larger culture today, either within the Church or outside of it, it is not much easier today to be a Kantian, a Balthasarian, a Marxist,

20. Jacques Maritain, *Distinguer pour Unir ou Les Degrés du Savoir* (Paris: Désclée de Brouwer, 1932); *The Degrees of Knowledge*, trans. G. B. Phelan (Notre Dame, IN: University of Notre Dame Press, 1995).

a logical positivist, or a Derridean, than it is to be a Thomistic Neo-Aristotelian. In this heterogeneous landscape, there is an increasingly level playing field, and in such a case as this, it is decidedly advantageous to have Thomas Aquinas on one's team.

So, what central issues does the Catholic Church face within our larger culture today? I have mentioned one above, which is the problem of the epistemic unity of the various academic and scientific disciplines in the modern university. We might briefly add a selective list of three others. First, no Catholic theology in the twentieth century seriously engaged with questions that arise from the discoveries of the modern scientific disciplines of physics, chemistry, and biology. In particular, there was very little theological engagement with the modern scientific narrative of the cosmos, one that arises from the considerations of contemporary big bang cosmology and evolutionary biology. This means that Catholic theology has ignored one of the core foundations of the modern university. Today, these disciplines stand at the center of academic culture, because they produce technologically useful knowledge for the economy and receive research grants and professionally oriented students from all cultures. The natural sciences are an inadequate intellectual lingua franca, but they do in fact play that role in the university life of the world today. And those who would advocate for a militant secularism—a "new atheism"—typically claim to be the true advocates of science, as if this new universal culture of the sciences should vindicate a new universal culture of secularism. And yet even at the same time, it is quite unclear within the larger university culture what philosophy might be employed to rightly interpret the discoveries of the modern scientific revolution. Analytic philosophy has no common doctrinal core to employ to decipher the significance of the natural sciences or to interpret human nature and our ethical life in relation to the explosion of modern scientific learning. The university remains theoretically disoriented so long as this is the case. Twentieth century Thomists of the River Forest school claimed that Thomism could offer a needed philosophical grounding to the study of modern physics, as well as an appreciation of the contributions evolutionary biology and psychological neuroscience for an understanding of the human being, while still underscoring the uniqueness of the spiritual principle in the human person and the importance of metaphysics for a philosophical understanding of the doctrine of creation.[21] Modern analytic philosophers typically want to see themselves as the philosophers who truly serve and facilitate the emergence of the scientific age, but they also struggle incessantly to understand basic problems of causation and capacity, natural kinds or essences, cosmic order, the unity of living forms, animal sentience, intentionality, and human rationality.[22] In the spirit of River Forest Thomism, there is a wonderful opportunity for a younger generation of Thomists to weigh in on these topics philosophically and theologically, for the good of the Church and the health of the greater culture at large.

Second, sexuality and gender. The teachings of the Church that will remain most contested in modern western culture are those that challenge directly the lifestyle changes that have emerged from the sexual revolution. Increasingly they mark out Catholic Christians as unintelligible subjects in the modern secular state and even as potential enemies. Here we have only to name fundamental teachings that we know are frequently misunderstood or dismissed: the dignity of human life from conception to natural death (in a culture in which abortion and euthanasia are increasingly commonplace and even seemingly banal), marriage as the morally appropriate context of sexual love, the heterosexual and procreative character of sexuality, the intrinsically problematic character of contraception, the perennial value of the celibate priesthood, the all-male priesthood as a complement in

---

21. See, most notably, Benedict Ashley, *The Way toward Wisdom: An Interdisciplinary and Intercultural Introduction to Metaphysics* (Notre Dame, IN: University of Notre Dame Press, 2006), and William A. Wallace, *The Modeling of Nature: Philosophy of Science and Philosophy of Nature in Synthesis* (Washington, DC: The Catholic University of America Press, 1996).

22. See the contemporary discussions in the context of analytic philosophy by David S. Oderberg, *Real Essentialism* (New York: Routledge, 2007), and Thomas Nagel, *Mind and Cosmos: Why the Materialist Neo-Darwinian Conception of Nature Is Almost Certainly False* (New York: Oxford University Press, 2012).

the life of the Church to feminine consecrated religious life. In addition, we might note the expanding set of bioethical issues where many cultures embrace practices that the Church cannot condone: in vitro fertilization, same-sex adoption, the morning-after pill, and prenatal eugenics. Such practices are becoming statistically normal.

These neuralgic issues are all related in some way to the theme of sexuality and gender. They touch upon the very nature of the human person as an animal who is capable of serving God in his or her body, as an inherently political animal who is born into and cared for by a family of persons, and who is also a fallen human being, in many ways wounded and weak, capable of sexual disorientation or of an almost religious obsession with sexuality, one that can in turn rival the claims of the transcendent God. This modern, hypersexualized human being is a being in need of mercy and compassion, and he or she can discover God precisely in the difficulties that arise from the complicated world of human sexuality. We need to discuss such topics, but we also need to resituate their consideration within a deeper treatment of the human person as a spiritual animal, bound by the inextinguishable desire for happiness, capable of developing the virtues, and of serving God in the body, capable of knowing the profound peace that comes only from the internal governance in all things by human spiritual love. Clearly, we cannot simply ignore such topics, either individually or in our respective religious orders, and hope that they disappear or that someone else who is braver than we will deal with them. In the past one has asked the question of how Catholic intellectuals could effectively change the dominant views of the mainstream culture by appeal to their own ethical tradition, but today it is increasingly a question of whether the dominant culture will even allow Catholics to articulate and practice what they traditionally believe.

It may seem that on these difficult subjects, Catholic theologians and philosophers lack sufficient allies in the wider non-Christian culture. That is true to be sure. However, the permissive world we live in also gradually gives rise to many profoundly disillusioned, wounded people, who are looking for a deeper moral formation on a variety of the above-mentioned contested issues. If theologians working within the Thomistic tradition provide a framework that is at once coherent and demanding but also rationally accessible and compassionate, we will be preparing a counter-alternative to the predominant culture, as a kind of potent intellectual remnant. We have at our disposal in this regard the great resources of Aquinas's account of the human person, as body and soul, spirit and sense, and his accompanying teleological conception of freedom, eudaimonistic ethics, and virtue theory. If this is articulated in a way that is accessible, rationally sensible, and authentically spiritual, it is powerful and compelling.

Lastly, dogmatic theology today lacks unity in the way that it explains the central mysteries of the Christian faith. Marie-Dominique Chenu sought to remedy this by referring to Aquinas's *exitus-reditus* schema: all that is found in creation and in the economy of salvation comes forth from God and all returns to him.[23] Chenu sought to read Aquinas's *Summa* in this way so as to procure for our own historically minded era a Thomistic theology of the divine economy and of human history. On Chenu's reading of Aquinas, dogmatic theology is a kind of meta-history. What should one make of this approach? Surely it should be said that modern historical studies in scripture, patristics, medieval, and modern thought, and in the domain of Thomism itself, have greatly enriched the intellectual patrimony of our time, and such studies are in some sense essential to a healthy theology. They provide us with intellectual orientation so that we may better perceive the intellectual conditions of the historical time in which revelation was received and composed and in which subsequent doctrinal traditions developed, as well as the intellectual landscape of our own era. All this can readily lead to speculative knowledge, since the recovery of the past opens us up to a principled, profound analysis of reality as it has been rightly understood by our forebears. Historical study is not at enmity with speculative theology, when rightly understood. However, it is also the case that

23. Marie-Dominique Chenu, *Toward Understanding Saint Thomas*, 304–14.

we live in a time in which the study of the structure of the mystery of the faith is itself neglected. Just what does it mean to speak about creation, not merely as a historical topic of medieval theology but as the foundational reality of our very being? What is the meaning of the Old Law as related to the New for the Church and for humanity? What is justification and how does it relate to merit? How ought we to understand the metaphysics of the Incarnation or the instrumental causality of the sacraments? We can study these questions in a historical optic, to be sure, and we can do so in the service of a Catholic Thomistic theology as such. But at some point one must address such questions as truth questions, and truth be told, today academic theology in many quarters is largely in the habit not so much of answering the questions constructively but of rehearsing the historical opinions accurately. It is a mistake to try to overcorrect in the other direction. What we need is a historically sound approach to the Bible, the Fathers, the medievals, and the moderns, but one which also seeks to find the speculative answers to the deepest theological questions, and to present those to persons of our time, in a unified and coherent way. That is to say, we need a living Thomistic dogmatic theology. This is especially the case when it comes to teaching seminarians, future priests, and religious: those who stand most acutely in existential need of a grounding in authentic theology and in the contemplation of the mystery of God. In stating things in this fashion, I am merely repeating what one finds in *Optatam totius*, §16: "Ultimately, in order to throw as full a light as possible on the mysteries of salvation, students should learn to examine more deeply, through speculative labor, and with St. Thomas as [master], all aspects of the [Christian] mysteries, and to perceive their interconnection." One thing we can do as a service to the vitality of theology in our own age, then, is to preserve the classical practice of theology as a science that peers into the mysteries of the faith, in their unity and inner intelligibility, as they cast light on one another. This scientific and contemplative or sapiential character of theology is most essential to the intellectual life of the Church.

CONCLUSION: CHRISTIAN INTELLECTUAL
VITALITY IN A SECULARIZED SOCIETY

Pope Paul VI claimed that in the modern age, people will believe in the Gospel when they see people giving their lives for it. There can be little doubt that we live in an age that gives more importance to witness of life than to intellectual argument. This idea of the primacy of practical witness can seem to be one we might juxtapose to the notion of a revival of Thomism. However, that need not be the case, especially if one considers the matter in a historical light. Scholasticism was a form of thought that developed in large part in religious communities of the thirteenth to the seventeenth centuries, and was employed to sustain not only the life of those communities but also their missionary activity across the span of the world. When Franciscans were formed in the thought of Bonaventure or Scotus, and Jesuits in the thought of Suárez or Vasquez, this formation was meant to equip them to engage with all facets of reality in the religious life in Europe and abroad. What their theological education aimed at was an integrated life of religious witness, one that included a profound speculative analysis of reality understood in light of God the Most Holy Trinity. This witness and the education it implied were meant to be carried to the farthest reaches of the world, and one should not forget what these religious orders truly accomplished, as they did undertake the most far reaching geographical missionary effort in the history of the Church, planting churches and true knowledge of Christ on every continent, grounded in their own personal witness to Christ. That integrity of spiritual life and intellectual vision, then, is something precious, and, it must be said, increasingly rare. Today we see very few Franciscan Bonaventurians or Jesuit Suarezians. And yet, amazingly, what I am referring to still subsists in the Church, where the speculative study of Thomism can still be found as something integrated within an evangelical witness of religious life, be it Dominican, Benedictine, Carmelite, or rooted in one of the many new religious orders that take Aquinas as their particular intellectual patron. It is also true in the diocesan seminary culture in the Church where Aquinas serves as a mentor for the acquisition of a balanced intellectual and spiritual life, in devotion to Christ at the heart of the Church, in view of the universal mission of the priesthood.

The era of postconciliar opprobrium regarding Thomism today is receding. It is time to engage anew, without trying to return to the now sterile debates about Thomism that took place in the immediate aftermath of the Council. Our context is different. We are called upon to serve the Church and to evangelize in a largely de-Christianized world. In this task, those who are priests, religious, and lay scholars have a certain responsibility for the intellectual life of the Catholic Church that cannot be ignored or delegated to others. But that responsibility is also a blessing: it has the power to shape our lives in wonderful ways as persons consecrated to the truth. It can be a source of new life within our own communities and for those to whom we preach or teach. By engaging in the study and promotion of the Thomistic tradition, we should hope confidently in the providence of God and his intrinsically effective grace, which our own intellectual tradition so rightly underscores. If members of the Church's intelligentsia seek with God's grace to promote the wisdom of the Angelic Doctor, God will fructify their meager efforts. It is for us to act with hope and to find inventive ways to do so together, now and in the future. The revitalization of Thomism will succeed best where it is lived out within the context of a dynamic religious and sacramental life committed to evangelical preaching. First, then: the integrity of the principles. Second: the vitality of contemporary engagement with the thought-world of our age. Third: the aspiration to live this out within the context of a dynamic ecclesial and sacramental life. Those are plausible aims for a living Thomism after Vatican II.

5

Ressourcement Thomism

Ressourcement Thomism refers to an emergent trend of theologians who seek to reassess the contribution of Thomas Aquinas both within his historical context and in a contemporary context. It is best explained genealogically in relation to other recent theological movements, and it has distinctive characteristics. In this final chapter I seek first to identify this historical context and characteristics of Ressourcement Thomism and then to illustrate its relevance by examining two typical theological claims found among those associated with the movement. The first of these is the claim that the modern focus on the "immanent and economic trinity" after Karl Rahner is conceptually problematic and that the Thomistic distinction between Trinitarian processions and Trinitarian missions serves as the more feasible one for a reasonable analysis of the way that the mystery of the Trinity is revealed in the economy of salvation. The latter model allows one to acknowledge more perfectly the New Testament revelation of the transcendence and unity of the Trinity and to avoid problematic historicizations of the divine life of God. The second claim is that key figures in modern kenotic theology, such as Karl Barth and Hans Urs von Balthasar, despite their theological creativity, have failed to preserve a sufficient sense of the distinction of the divine and human natures in Christ. Aquinas's

Chalcedonian and dyothelitist Christology provides theologians with ways of thinking about how the crucifixion of God reveals the mystery of the Trinity in and through the sufferings of Christ without the problematic projection of human characteristics of the Lord onto the inner life of the Trinity, as constitutive of the inner life of the Trinity. In both these respects Ressourcement Thomism as a theological movement suggests ways that historical theology concerned with the contribution of patristic and medieval sources can lead to a renewal of and creative engagement in modern theology.

RESSOURCEMENT THOMISM IN CONTEXT

Ressourcement Thomism is perhaps best understood against the backdrop of three antecedent intellectual movements, which are positioned both chronologically and logically in reaction to one another. I am referring here first chronologically to Leonine Thomism, second to the *Nouvelle théologie* movement initiated by Henri de Lubac and Jean Daniélou in the 1940s, and third to the *Thomasian* movement of historical study of Aquinas in his medieval context, represented by figures such as Étienne Gilson, Marie-Dominique Chenu, and Jean-Pierre Torrell.

The first of these movements, broadly understood, refers to the initiative undertaken by Pope Leo XIII in his 1879 encyclical letter *Aeterni Patris*, which called for the renewal of scholastic theological and philosophical studies in the Catholic Church in response to the onset of secularizing philosophies issued from influential Enlightenment authors and from the social revolutions of the nineteenth century. The movement to which this initiative gave rise was widespread, creating new centers of medieval scholarship and Thomistic thought in places like Rome, Leuven, Toulouse, Fribourg, and eventually in a number of centers in North and South America, such as Toronto and Santiago. From the 1870s to the 1950s Catholic theology in Europe was characteristically scholastic in tone, as represented by thinkers like Johann Baptist Franzelin, Matthias Joseph Scheeben,

Réginald Garrigou-Lagrange, Michel Labourdette, Jacques Maritain, and Charles Journet. In response to Enlightenment criticisms of
Christianity, this movement placed great emphasis on philosophical
formation in metaphysics and epistemology, the reasonableness of
belief in God, the logical possibility of divine revelation, the intelligibility of the mysteries of Christianity, and the Christian mystical
life as one superior to that of purely natural reason.

The *Nouvelle théologie* movement was inaugurated by de Lubac
and Daniélou and can be dated symbolically by their creation of a
famous series of patristic translations, *Sources Chrétiennes*, in 1942.
Critically speaking they reacted against what they took to be a too
narrow focus in modern Catholic theology on scholastic philosophy, definitions, and arguments. Modern scholasticism, as they saw
it, often lacked sufficient historical consciousness, engagement with
contemporary philosophy and literature, cultural urbanity, and existential and spiritual relevance to modern persons. Where Leonine
theology relied heavily on classical philosophy and argumentative
demonstrations, they sought to retrieve and re-appropriate a patristic model of exegesis of Scripture as a propaedeutic to theology, with emphasis on the spiritual senses of Scripture. De Lubac's
famous work *Surnaturel* (1946) was controversial not only because
of its thesis (of a natural appetite in all persons for the supernatural)
but also because it advanced a new way of studying Aquinas in historical context, and it suggested that were one to do so, central tenets of thinking about grace and nature in subsequent "Thomistic"
theology should be revised or overturned. De Lubac's theology was
more historical in method, associative in theme rather than argumentative, and culturally engaged within a modern secular context.
It sought in its own way to establish Catholic theology as a normative thought-form within a modern European intellectual context.
The movement was of major influence during the Second Vatican
Council and in the papacies of John Paul II and Benedict XVI, both
of whom were in diverse ways influenced by the movement.

The *Thomasian* movement of historical studies developed in

great part from the example of mid-20th century medievalists like Gilson and Chenu who sought to resituate Aquinas within his original context so as to apprehend his original insights and contribution to the patrimony of Christian thought. In differentiation from Leonine scholasticism, this vein of modern Thomism has tended to treat Aquinas primarily as a theologian, rather than as a philosopher, and as an interpreter of Scripture and patristic tradition, with a view toward the assimilation of the Aristotelian and classical philosophical heritage. In regard to its method of reading Aquinas, this movement has taken inspiration from the *Nouvelle théologie* movement in many respects. However, it has done so in order to maintain a privileged role for Aquinas's thought within Christian theological venues, and in this respect it maintains some of the aims of the Leonine revival. In differentiation from that movement, however, theologians associated with the historical study of Aquinas in the post-Vatican II period tend to focus on Aquinas as a dogmatician, spiritual teacher, and exegete, rather than as a metaphysician. Where the Leonine authors tended to treat "the Thomistic tradition" as a theoretical set of principles maintained in continuity by Thomists down through the ages, *Thomasian* scholars are more likely to treat Aquinas's teaching historically with a view toward inspiring contemporary projects, but not per se so as to extract a living form of teaching from Aquinas for promotion in the modern context. As a historical project this movement is more conservationist than innovational, and its practitioners may eschew constructive proposals concerning the objective content of a "Thomistic tradition."

In many respects Ressourcement Thomism has come out of the latter movement, making use of its resources of examining Aquinas in medieval context. Its typical practitioners do so, however, so as to re-assert the idea of a viable and ongoing Thomistic intellectual tradition, and therefore they tend to treat the commentatorial tradition of Renaissance and baroque "Thomists" (like Thomas de Vio Cajetan, and Domingo Báñez) as an additional historical resource and subject of study. By attempting to promote principles of Thomistic thought within a contemporary context, members of this movement resemble practitioners of the Leonine revival. However, in similitude to the *Nouvelle théologie*, this movement tends to place emphasis on the centrality of Aquinas's exegesis and patristic influences, as well as engagement with contemporary non-Thomistic and non-Christian intellectual thought forms. In this sense Ressourcement Thomism could be said to result sociologically from a selective synthesis of influences of these past three movements. In a way that is different from the other three movements, it has a consistent and wide ecumenical scope, engaging Protestant scripture scholars and theologians and even theoretical questions of what authentic and reasonable ecumenicism consists in.

Initial sources of inspiration for this movement would include Servais Pinckaers, Alasdair MacIntyre, and Romanus Cessario, whose writings in ethics center on virtue theory.[1] They undertook a genealogical analysis of how virtue theory emerged in patristic and medieval Christian thought, noted how it was largely neglected as a resource in modern ethics, and identified key elements of Aquinas's theory of personal agency, moral objects and ends, grace and freedom, virtue and vice. They undertook this analysis while placing Aquinas's normative claims in conversation with contemporary alternatives, typically arguing that his principles are more explanatory and intellectually compelling than alternative theories. Following this methodological stance, historical *ressourcement* is aimed eventually at the retrieval and identification of principal truth claims that in turn need to be demonstrated to have superior explanatory power in comparison with contemporary alternatives. Only then are the

1. Servais Pinckaers, *The Sources of Christian Ethics*, 3rd ed., trans. M. T. Noble (Washington, DC: The Catholic University of America Press, 1995); Alasdair MacIntyre, *After Virtue: A Study in Moral Theory*, 3rd ed. (Notre Dame, IN: University of Notre Dame Press, 1997); MacIntyre, *Three Rival Versions of Moral Inquiry* (London: Bloomsbury, 1990); MacIntyre, *First Principles, Final Ends, and Contemporary Philosophical Issues* (Milwaukee,: Marquette University Press, 1990); Romanus Cessario, *Introduction to Moral Theology*, rev. ed. (Washington, DC: The Catholic University of America Press, 2013); Cessario, *The Moral Virtues and Theological Ethics*, 2nd ed. (Notre Dame, IN: University of Notre Dame Press, 2008).

principles both understood sufficiently from within their original historical context and deployed in a sufficiently intellectually compelling way within the horizon of contemporary culture.[2]

Based on this core idea, we can detail common proposals of the Ressourcement Thomistic movement by paying attention to themes found in the work of some of its key figures. First and foremost, Matthew Levering has sought to identify Aquinas's theological method by returning to his conception of *sacra doctrina*, or theology as a discipline of biblical explanation.[3] Read in this way, Aquinas is primarily a scriptural theologian, with patristic commitments, who makes use of metaphysical and philosophical reflection in subordination to his interpretation of Scripture. Levering's Thomism seeks to narrow the divide between scholastic and historical-critical forms of modern theology by both centering on the reading of sources and insisting on the essential importance of metaphysics as a dimension of Christian doctrine.[4] He also seeks to employ Aquinas's dialectical method of scholastic treatment of opinions in a contemporary context by comparing Aquinas's own theological ideas with a host of modern alternatives, seeking to manifest their potential veracity by comparing Thomistic options with those represented by other schools. Levering founded the quintessential Ressourcement Thomism journal, the English edition of *Nova et Vetera*, and is co-editor of an influential series of monographs published under the title from which the movement is named.

Serge-Thomas Bonino, Gilles Emery, and Bruce D. Marshall are other emblematic figures whose respective works on the mystery of

2. See MacIntyre's argument to this effect in *First Principles, Final Ends, and Contemporary Philosopical Issues* (1990), and *Three Rival Versions of Moral Inquiry* (1990), 196–215.

3. Matthew Levering, *Engaging the Doctrine of Revelation* (Grand Rapids, MI: Baker Academic, 2014); Levering, *Scripture and Metaphysics: Aquinas and the Renewal of Trinitarian Theology* (Oxford: Wiley-Blackwell, 1994).

4. See the arguments to this effect in Levering, *Participatory Biblical Exegesis: A Theology of Biblical Interpretation* (Notre Dame, IN: University of Notre Dame Press, 2008) and Levering, *Engaging the Doctrine of Creation: Cosmos, Creatures, and the Wise and Good Creator* (Grand Rapids, MI: Baker Academic, 2017).

God and the Trinity are especially influential. Bonino has composed what is simultaneously a thorough historical study and theoretical defense of the classical "divine names" treatise in Aquinas, the *de Deo Uno* treatment of the divine attributes in *Summa theologiae* I, qq. 2–26.[5] In his analysis of divine simplicity, perfection, eternity, immutability, omnipresence, providence and so on, Bonino challenges the normative character of trends in post-Hegelian kenotic theology (as found, for example, in Jürgen Moltmann or Sergius Bulgakov) as well as contemporary analytic revisionist theology that often places God in time as a mutable subject living in co-simultaneous duration with creatures (as found, for example, in Richard Swinburne or William Hasker). Emery, meanwhile, has had great influence in rehabilitating the historical study of medieval Trinitarian theology with a view toward its uses in a modern theological context. His study of the notions in Aquinas of processions, relations, persons, and modes of Trinitarian presence of God to the world, especially in divine missions, is of widespread influence. It offers contemporary theologians an idiom in which to consider the way God subsists in himself and reveals himself to the world, as a counter-alternative to the theologies of Barth, Rahner, and von Balthasar (a point I will return to below).[6] Bruce Marshall has underscored similar themes, employing Aquinas's theology of God to critique formulations of divine suffering that are present in contemporary Trinitarian theology.[7] In light of the classical doctrine of divine unity, Marshall has also presented argumentation against those who would claim that the persons in God acquire their identity in virtue of their relations to creatures

5. Serge-Thomas Bonino, *Dieu, "Celui Qui Est"- De Deo ut Uno* (Paris: Parole et Silence, 2016). [Translation forthcoming in English, Thomistic Ressourcement Series, The Catholic University of America Press.]

6. Gilles Emery, *The Trinitarian Theology of St. Thomas Aquinas*, trans. F. Murphy (Oxford: Oxford University Press, 2010); Emery, *Trinity, Church, and the Human Person* (Naples, FL: Sapientia Press, 2007); Emery, *Trinity in Aquinas* (Naples, FL: Sapientia Press, 2006).

7. Bruce D. Marshall, "The Dereliction of Christ and the Impassibility of God," in *Divine Impassibility and the Mystery of Human Suffering*, ed. J. Keating and T. J. White (Grand Rapids, MI: Eerdmans, 2009), 246–98.

or that they come to relate to one another in new ways, supposedly, on the basis of what they do or suffer progressively in the economy of salvation.[8]

Simon Gaine, Thomas Joseph White, and Dominic Legge have produced substantive Christological treatises that stand largely in logical congruity with the work of Bonino, Emery, and Marshall.[9] They have in diverse ways sought to present Aquinas's Christological claims anew with a view toward their modern relevance. Gaine and White have defended, in different ways, the traditional teaching that Christ enjoyed the beatific vision, or the immediate knowledge of God, in the heights of his human intellect during the time of his earthly life, in such a way that he knew clearly of his own identity as the Son of God in a fully human way, expressing this knowledge in the cultural and linguistic terms of his day. White has underscored the importance of Aquinas's single-subject Christology in critical engagement with the Christology of Rahner, which he characterizes as leaning toward Nestorianism. Legge, meanwhile, has employed Aquinas's doctrine of Trinitarian missions to underscore how Jesus's human life reveals the Trinity, in critical dialogue with Rahner's theology of the economic Trinity.

Richard Schenk, Reinhard Hütter, Bernhard Blankenhorn, and Lawrence Feingold have each in various ways presented contemporary Thomistic proposals in theological anthropology.[10] Schenk's

8. Bruce D. Marshall, "Personal Distinction in God and the Possibility of Kenosis," *Angelicum* 98, no. 1 (2021): 65–104; Marshall, "The Absolute and the Trinity," *Pro Ecclesia* 23, no. 2 (2014): 147–64; Marshall, "The Unity of the Triune God: Reviving an Ancient Question," *The Thomist* 74 (2010): 1–32.

9. Simon Francis Gaine, *Did the Saviour See the Father? Christ, Salvation, and the Vision of God* (London: T&T Clark, 2015); Thomas Joseph White, *The Incarnate Lord: A Thomistic Study in Christology* (Washington, DC: The Catholic University of America Press, 2015), Dominic Legge, *The Trinitarian Christology of St. Thomas Aquinas* (Oxford: Oxford University Press, 2016).

10. Richard Schenk, *Soundings in the History of a Hope: New Studies on Thomas Aquinas* (Naples, FL: Sapientia Press, 2016); Schenk, *Revelations of Humanity Anthropological Dimensions of Theological Controversies* (Washington, DC: The Catholic University of America Press, 2022); Hütter, *Bound for Beatitude: A Thomistic Study in Eschatology and Ethics* (Washington, DC: The Catholic University of America Press, 2019); Reinhard Hütter, *Dust Bound for Heaven: Explorations in the Theology of Thomas Aquinas,* (Grand Rapids,

work centers on Aquinas's Aristotelian, hylomorphic conception of human persons, read in his original medieval context against the backdrop of Augustinian anthropology. He presents Aquinas in dialogue above all with Augustine, Luther, Heidegger, and Rahner, arguing that St. Thomas's realism regarding the tragedy of death and the reality of human finitude invites one to understand the gratuity of the grace of faith in a way that speaks to the concerns of these modern thinkers, while presenting at the same time a superior anthropology of human embodiment and Christ-centered sacramental dependence. Hütter has produced a project of the study of teleology in theological anthropology, arguing that Aquinas's analysis of eschatological beatitude provides him with a key point of orientation for interpreting the meaning of human existence, one that has increasing relevance in an era of metaphysical disorientation. In a way that parallels MacIntyre, Hütter argues that Thomistic metaphysics and anthropology can play a key role for modern theology when it is confronted with the twin challenges of postmodern philosophical skepticism and biological material reductionism. Thomism has a superior explanatory power when one seeks to understand personal identity within the modern context. Blankenhorn has made use of extensive study of Aquinas's doctrine of the gifts of the Holy Spirit in its original historical context to argue for a profound harmony of the natural and supernatural orders, and of the grace of faith with natural intellectual insight, against the backdrop of what he argues is a tendency toward "grace-nature extrinsicism" in the theology of the gifts as interpreted by John of St. Thomas and Garrigou-Lagrange. Lawrence Feingold has produced what is no doubt one of the most controversial works of contemporary Catholic theology. Making use of the historical-critical study of sources in a way that is emblematic of the *Nouvelle théologie*, he revisits the theological sources employed by de Lubac in *Surnaturel* in order to argue for an alternative read-

MI: Eerdmans, 2012); Lawrence Feingold, *The Natural Desire to See God according to St. Thomas Aquinas and His Interpreters*, 2nd ed. (Naples, FL: Sapientia Press, 2010); Bernhard Blankenhorn, *The Mystery of Union with God: Dionysian Mysticism in Albert the Great and Thomas Aquinas* (Washington, DC: The Catholic University of America Press, 2015).

ing of Aquinas on the natural desire for God, one that is concordant with subsequent Thomistic commentators such as Sylvester of Ferrara. Feingold carries this commentatorial tradition forward to argue for its conceptual superiority to both that of de Lubac in his theology of the absolute desire for the supernatural and that of Rahner in his supernatural-existential theology of grace, in which grace is always already a co-compositional principle with human nature.

There are also characteristic Ressourcement Thomist treatments of topics in ecclesiology and sacramental theology. Benoit-Dominique de la Soujeole has produced a series of major studies of the mystery of the Church, which are of Thomistic inspiration and that make use of the thought of Journet.[11] De la Soujeole interprets the teaching of the Second Vatican Council that the Church is a "sign and instrument of salvation" in light of Aquinas's understanding of sacraments, distinguishing the *sacramentum tantum* of the Church, the *res et sacramentum*, and the *res tantum*.[12] In this schema, the first term designates the visible ecclesial means of salvation instituted by Christ in view of the eschaton. The second designates the visible Church now living mysteriously the eschatological life to come, while the third designates the mystery of plenary salvation in the eschaton, in which all those who are currently invisible members of Christ will be manifest as part of the visible life of the Church. Correspondingly, Emmanuel Perrier has produced reflection on human agency as a nexus-concept in Aquinas's theology that allows one to understand Christ's human agency, its role in our redemption in concord with the theology of human action under grace, and our active participation in the sacraments, which function as a medium of grace.[13] Christ's human instrumental agency

---

11. Benoit-Dominique de la Soujeole, *Introduction to the Mystery of the Church*, trans. M. J. Miller (Washington, DC: The Catholic University of America Press, 2016); Benoit-Dominique de la Soujeole, *Le sacrement de la communion: essai d'ecclésiologie fondamentale* (Paris: Cerf, 1998).

12. De la Soujeole, *Introduction to the Mystery of the Church*, 438–96.

13. Emmanuel Perrier, *L'attrait divin: La doctrine de l'opération et le gouvernement des créatures chez saint Thomas d'Aquin* (Paris: Parole et Silence, 2019).

and the instrumentality of the sacraments are not opposed to genuine human freedom under grace but rather are the condition for it. Reginald Lynch has studied Thomistic sacramental theology of the post-Reformation era to examine how Aquinas's notion of sacraments as instrumental causes of grace and his theology of the Mass as a sacrifice were taken up and developed in the early modern context.[14] Thomistic theories of sacramental causality in the baroque era offered answers to objections from alternative Catholic schools that anticipate the critical objections of "post-metaphysical" sacramental theologians in contemporary theology influenced by Martin Heidegger and modern phenomenology.

What becomes manifest in this tapestry of examples is the recent emergence of a thematic form of Thomism, one that seeks to advance principles and normative claims derived from the theology of Aquinas and his traditional interpreters. In differentiation from the earlier Leonine Thomism, this form of theology is more historical in method and more overtly theological and exegetical, with an eye toward the spiritual and existential horizon of Aquinas's thought. It is more committed to the enduring importance of the scholastic heritage of Christian theology than authors associated with the *Nouvelle théologie* but expresses that commitment against the backdrop of postmodern hermeneutics, geneological historicism, and methodological pluralism in modern theology. It is more robustly metaphysical in orientation than the *Thomasian* movement, and it is more critically engaged in making contemporary theological claims but does so without characterizing the latter movement as inessential or problematic. On the contrary, in the thought form characteristic of the above mentioned authors, the historical study of Aquinas typically plays a key role as an irreplaceable moment within a larger process of retrieval and re-articulation of Thomistic principles in a contemporary idiom.

14. Reginald Lynch, *The Cleansing of the Heart: The Sacraments as Instrumental Causes in the Thomistic Tradition* (Washington, DC: The Catholic University of America Press, 2017).

FROM THE ECONOMIC TRINITY TO
PROCESSIONS AND MISSIONS

As an illustration of theses typical of theologians associated with Ressourcement Thomism it is helpful to consider two examples, the first pertaining to the theology of Trinitarian processions and missions and the second pertaining to the theology of the two natures of Christ. In each case, analysis of what Aquinas argued in his original historical context can be seen to be of potential assistance to contemporary theological discernment.

Trinitarian theology in the twentieth century has no doubt been marked quintessentially by the exploration of Rahner's *Grundaxiom*, the idea that the immanent Trinity is the economic Trinity and vice versa.[15] The idea seemingly has its origins in Barth's *Church Dogmatics* I, 1, where Barth sought to place the Trinity at the center of his treatment of revelation and in doing so assigned reasons for the distinction of the persons in God to the diverse economic functions or activities of the persons.[16] The Father is characterized, for example, as the revealer, the Son as the one revealed in the human life of Christ, and the Spirit as the immanent source of the revealing in human history, the one who manifests Christ as the Son and in doing so, manifests the original source of revelation who is the Father.[17] This idea could be defended by recourse to the classical theology of Trinitarian attribution, in which each of the persons always acts together, but in such a way that each one is revealed more particularly by some of their common actions.[18] (As indeed, the Father, Son and Spirit can act co-simultaneously so as to reveal one person in particular, the crucified Jesus as Lord, for example.) Barth's formulation is more ambiguous, however, since his presentation raises the question

15. Karl Rahner, *The Trinity*, trans. J. Donceel (London: Continuum, 2001), esp. 22.

16. Karl Barth, *Church Dogmatics* [CD], trans. and ed. G. W. Bromiley and T. F. Torrance, 4 vols. (Edinburgh: T&T Clark, 1936–75). I, 1 (1936–75).

17. Barth, *CD* I, 1, 306–34.

18. See, for example, Aquinas, *ST* I, q. 38, aa. 7–8, who appeals to expressions and ideas taken from Paul, Augustine, Abelard, and Peter Lombard.

of whether God the Trinity is characterized "always already," i.e. eternally, by relations of the Trinitarian persons to creatures in virtue of divine election, covenant, and redemptive incarnation. Barth's later theology of election (*CD* II,2), of the *analogia relationis* (*CD* III, 3), and of Christ's filial dereliction (*CD*, IV, 1) augments the tension in this perspective, as it is possible to understand the identity of the Trinity in historical terms, as a mystery of three persons eternally self-determined by and in the decision for relationality to creation.[19]

Rahner offers his own creative appropriation and reinterpretation of Barth's somewhat open-ended idea. Rahner claims that the economic activity of the Trinity is characterized by real relations of the distinct persons to human beings to whom the revelation of God is addressed.[20] This implies that God self-determines in view of the economy, and he does so differently in each person. Rahner also distances his account from any reliance upon the traditional theology of the attributes of the divine nature (pertaining to the unity of God as such), or that of the psychological analogy (of the Son as Word and the Spirit as Love) to characterize the immanent Trinity.[21] What results is a theology in which one can only intelligibly understand the real distinction of the persons in God from their distinct activities in the economy of revelation, in which they communicate divine life to humanity by grace. Rahner maintains that this economic life of God's three persons present in the world corresponds to what God is immanently and eternally, but the expression of this idea is inevitably ambiguous. Does Rahner mean that we know from revelation that the historical act of self-communication of God corresponds to what God is and would be as Trinity independently of creation, or does he mean that God is himself not only in virtue of this "pre-creation" identity but also only always because of his economic history as one present among us? Regardless of how one interprets Rahner on this score, his position inspired intellectual succes-

---

19. See, for example, Barth, *CD* II, 2, 94–194; *CD* III, 3, 94–107; *CD* IV, 1, 157–357.
20. Rahner, *The Trinity*, 26–30.
21. Rahner, *The Trinity*, 10–21, 46–48, 115–20.

sors who sought to develop the latter interpretation. Moltmann, for example, understands the history of Christ crucified to take place, in some real respect, within the very being of God, so that the suffering and death of the Son as human is historically constitutive of the relational identity of the persons in God.[22] Von Balthasar, meanwhile, argues like Barth that whatever happens in the economy must have its precondition in the eternal identity of the Trinity. However, he adds the idea of a Trinitarian potentiality for development that occurs actually in the economy. From all eternity, in the immanent Trinity, the Spirit proceeds from the Father and the Son. However, in the economy the order is inverted. In the life of Jesus, the Spirit precedes the Son and sends him, so that God adopts internally a distinct order of personal processions for the sake of the redemption. It is inverted once again when the redemption is accomplished, but in the process, the immanent Trinity undergoes ontological enrichment in virtue of its economic history.[23]

Without denying the remarkable creativity and modern intellectual verve of these projects, authors associated with Ressourcement Thomism typically seek to preserve key insights and elements of classical Trinitarian theology. This is notably the case with regard to the theology of divine processions, relations, and persons, the employment of the psychological analogy, and the regulatory role of a theology of the divine attributes (divine simplicity, perfection, eternity, immutability, and so forth). Aquinas, for example, argues in light of the doctrine of divine simplicity that the persons of the Trinity are equally divine and therefore must each possess the fullness of the divine life and essence.[24] It follows that they are not distinguishable from one another personally in virtue of properties they exert

22. Jürgen Moltmann, *The Crucified God: The Cross of Christ as the Foundation and Criticism of Christian Theology*, trans. R. A. Wilson (San Francisco: Harper and Row, 1974), 200–78.

23. Hans Urs von Balthasar, *Theo-Drama Theological Dramatic Theory* III: *The Dramatis Personae: Persons in Christ*, trans. G. Harrison (San Francisco: Ignatius Press, 1993), 183–91 and 521–23.

24. Aquinas, *ST* I, q. 42, aa. 1–4.

as God in the economy of creation and salvation, but only in virtue of their eternal immanent processions from one another and the relations of opposition that arise therefrom.[25] The Father is eternally characterized by his paternal generation of the Word and spiration of the Spirit, just as the Word is characterized by his reception of all he is from the Father and by his spiration of the Spirit with the Father, while the Spirit is characterized by the eternal receptivity of all he is from the Father and Son as their mutually spirated Love.[26] As Emery has noted, what results from this conception of the immanent Trinity is a Thomistic notion of conceptual "redoubling" when thinking of the persons in God.[27] Each is wholly relational in all that he is (toward the other two persons), and each is wholly God. Without thinking of each of these aspects one cannot think rightly of any of the persons. What follows from this for one's theology of the economy is a three-fold idea. First, each person is constituted from all eternity by relations of origin, in virtue of the processions of generation of the Word and spiration of the Spirit, not by their historical relationships to creation. Second, in the economy of creation and redemption, each person only ever acts with the other two in all they do, so that no person acts by a divine power lacking to the other two. Yet each person also only ever acts in a distinct personal mode, that is to say in a way that is paternal, filial, or spirated, even when they act together. This means that the activity of God in the economy of grace does indeed reveal each person, as Rahner wishes to underscore, but it does so also by revealing the persons in their divine unity and perfection. When the persons act together by grace, for example, to reveal Jesus as Lord and eternal Son of God made man, they do so in such a way as to reveal the pre-existent Father of the Son, and the Spirit of the Father and Son as well.[28] Third, Aquinas follows Augustine in arguing from Scripture that the missions of the Trinitarian persons are distinct from their eternal processions but that

25. Aquinas, *ST* I, q. 29, a. 4.
26. Aquinas, *ST* I, qq. 27 and 28.
27. Emery, *Trinity in Aquinas*, 165–208.
28. Emery, *Trinity, Church, and the Human Person*, 115–54.

they reveal the processions, manifesting to us in time the true eternal identity of God.[29] Aquinas defines a mission of a divine person as an eternal procession with the addition of a temporal effect.[30] In other words, when the Son of God is sent by the Father (John 3:17; 17:18; 20:21) from all eternity into the world, his mission consists in the real ontological mystery of the Son in himself, as the eternally be-gotten Word, now rendered present to human beings in a new way, in virtue of his personal subsistence in a human nature, as one who is fully human. God therefore reveals himself in the "otherness" of human flesh, human activity and suffering, and even in human death and resurrection. The mission of God the Son among us is therefore truly revelatory of the eternal identity of God, but his temporal mis-sion is not constitutive of that identity.

It follows from this understanding of eternal processions and temporal missions that the relational order of the persons of God cannot evolve or change in virtue of the missions. The missions re-veal who God truly is. It is precisely for this reason that they cannot give rise to new intra-Trinitarian relations that would "re-constitute" God anew in himself, but rather they can only ever reflect who God truly is in himself antecedent to his redemption of the human race. Consequently the Balthasarian notion of the Trinitarian in-version seems problematic, as it would suggest that the identity of the persons that occurs in virtue of their mutual relations is mal-leable just in virtue of the modalities of divine action and suffering that occur in the economy. In this case God seems to be constitut-ed essentially as God by the economy. Meanwhile in light of Aqui-nas's approach, Rahner's famous claim that the Son alone could be-come incarnate appears problematic. Rahner argues that God must self-communicate in his Word and can only self-communicate per-fectly through incarnation, so that if God does create, the Word must become human.[31] It is true that the Son's mission from the Father

29. Aquinas, *ST* I, q. 43, which depends in part on the biblically based arguments of Augustine in *The Trinity*, IV, ch. 20.

30. Aquinas, *ST* I, q. 43, a. 2, ad 3.

31. Rahner, *The Trinity*, 29, 33.

reveals his eternal identity as Word and expresses this "outwardly" in the divine self-communication that takes place in virtue of the Incarnation. However, God could in principle manifest himself otherwise than he has (even if, as Aquinas argues, he has done so most fittingly through the Incarnation of the Word).[32] This freedom of God to save us in diverse ways must be the case if the processions "precede" the missions and are not determined in their ontological content by them, but on the contrary, determine the ontological content of them. God could have "sent" the Spirit in a form of manifestation that was analogous to that of the incarnation of the Son, even if he more fittingly sent the Son as his Word, in human nature. This possibility of an alternative economy is not a merely frivolous counter-factual thought experiment of scholastic theologians. The idea is bound up with the notion that the Trinity is eternally transcendent as Creator, preceding and giving rise to all that has being from God. Indeed each of the divine persons has the omnipotent capacity not only to create but also to become incarnate in human nature. Consequently the Trinity is free to self-unveil to humanity in a plurality of modes. If indeed God has chosen to do so in one distinct economic pattern (through the incarnation of the Son, in his crucifixion and resurrection, and in the visible sending of the Spirit at Pentecost), then the decision is not an arbitrary one but is one that must be inwardly marked by the wisdom and goodness of God, and thus it is intelligible to human thought.

Likewise, as Bruce Marshall as argued, if the Son's human suffering is genuinely indicative of the eternal love of the Trinity for the human race and revelatory of that love, it is not for that reason constitutive of the Trinitarian relations (pace Moltmann) nor need it mirror precisely (by a supposed analogy) the inner life of God as Triune.[33] That is to say, we are not obliged to infer from the suffering of the Son what the Son is eternally in his procession from the Fa-

32. Aquinas, *ST* III, q. 3, aa. 5 and 8. See the analysis of Legge, *Trinitarian Christology*, 61–102.

33. Marshall, "The Dereliction of Christ and the Impassibility of God," in *Divine Impassibility and the Mystery of Human Suffering.*

ther. The three persons are one in virtue of their shared nature and not in virtue of their ethical cooperation in the economy of the crucifixion and resurrection. In fact, their capacity to save the human race in and through Jesus's human life, suffering, and resurrection presupposes and depends upon their transcendent unity in wisdom, goodness, and free omnipotent love. It is because they possess this unity of love antecedent to the mystery of salvation, with its corresponding power, that they can be present and active within the event of atonement as the primal Creator, who is able to redeem the human race even from within the dark night of extraordinary suffering. It is this salvific mystery of the transcendent Trinity that is revealed to be immanently present and operative in the crucifixion, death, and resurrection of Christ.[34]

THE TWO NATURES OF CHRIST

Analogous themes emerge in Ressourcement Thomist authors who engage in contemporary debates in Christology. Undoubtedly in modern Christology of the past century, German-speaking Protestant and Catholic theologians alike have underscored kenotic themes. The famous dereliction theologies of Barth and von Balthasar, for example, have placed great emphasis on the Son's human obedience, suffering, and godforsakenness in the crucifixion as a particular locus of revelation of the divinity of the Son in his relation to the Father.[35] By an appeal to what he calls the *genus tapeinoticum* in the use of the communication of idioms, Barth asks to what extent the human attributes of Christ may be ascribed to his divine nature, to the Son in his mode of being as God.[36] This inquiry leads to the idea that there exists a likeness of similitude or analogy between the Son in his divine nature and the Son in his human nature, such that the human activ-

---

34. See the argument to this effect by White, *The Incarnate Lord*, 340–464.

35. This amounts to a creative re-interpretation of Luther's *theologia crucis*. See Barth, *CD* IV, 1, section 59, and von Balthasar, *Theo-Drama Theological-Dramatic Theory IV: The Action*, trans. G. Harrison (San Francisco: Ignatius Press, 1994), 319–28.

36. Barth, *CD* IV, 1, 215, 239, 264, 306, 308, 458, 566, 590; *CD* IV, 2, 84–85, 108–15.

ities of obedience, suffering, and free acceptance of abandonment correspond to something transcendent in the divine nature, making these human activities possible. The dereliction of Christ crucified reveals the inner capacity of the divine nature for self-emptying and suffering as motivated by divine love. Von Balthasar attempts to give thematic expression to this idea in the form of an *analogia entis Christi*: the analogy of being discovered in Christ, whereby the human freedom of love in Christ that leads him to embrace the abandonment by God on Holy Saturday is indicative of a mutual surrender and free exchange of separation and reconciliation that exists in the Trinity and in the life of God from all eternity.[37]

When one compares these ideas with the Christologies advanced by recent Thomists, points of convergence appear, as well as points of potential difference. Aquinas follows Maximus the Confessor and John Damascene in his interpretation of the Third Ecumenical Council of Constantinople, which affirmed that there are two natural wills and activities in Christ, as God and as human respectively. In interpreting this Council, Damascene underscored that the human nature of Jesus is the instrument of the divine person of the Son. This means that the activity of Christ's human mind and heart is distinct from and subordinate to his divine nature and activity. However, due to this same subordination, both his actions and sufferings, as one who is human, are wholly and genuinely expressive of his divine personal identity.[38]

Thomists have noted a number of parallels to and points of contact with the modern kenotic tradition that emerge from this standpoint. First, it follows from Aquinas's understanding that all that Christ is conscious of, and knows and wills as a human being, is expressive of his filial identity as the Son of God and of his relation to the Father and the Spirit.[39] Likewise, all that he suffers as man is ex-

37. Von Balthasar, *Theo-Logic Theological Logical Theory* II, *The Truth of God*, trans. A. Walker (San Francisco: Ignatius Press, 2004), 94–95, 128–34, 173–218, 273n109.

38. In *ST* III, q. 19, a. 1, Aquinas follows Damascene's interpretation of the Third Council of Chalcedon found in *On the Orthodox Faith*, III, c. 16.

39. See White, *The Incarnate Lord*, 236–74.

pressive of this same set of personal relationships. Jesus has a filial way of being human, because his human nature is the human nature of the Son subsisting as man. Consequently, just as the Son's divine nature is filial in its mode of being, as being eternally received from the Father, so too his human nature is filial in its mode of being, and expresses *in a human way* who he is personally as the Son. Therefore even when it is expressed in a distinctly human way rather than a divine way, Jesus's receptivity to the Father in obedience and suffering is indicative of his personal derivation of life from the Father.[40] On this reading, the human acts and sufferings of Christ in the crucifixion are indicative of the eternal identity of the Son in relation to the Father and the Spirit. However, obedience, suffering, and the experience of abandonment cannot be properly ascribed to the divine nature nor are they somehow constitutive of the Trinitarian persons in their eternal relations, even by a kind of faint analogy (of inner divine suffering or eternal poverty). The reason is that these features of being are rightly ascribed to the Son of God only in virtue of his human nature and as attributes pertaining uniquely to created dimensions of reality. The Trinity is not capable of eternal obedience, since the biblical concept of obedience implies created dependency, and a movement from imperfection to greater perfection acquired by ontological subordination to a superior principle.[41] The Father and the Son, however, are eternally one in divine perfection, power, and authority. The notion of obedience also implies free consent between two subjects with distinct wills. However, the Father, Son, and Spirit are one in essence (*homoousios*) and therefore also one in will. In fact there can be no free consent between persons in the Trinity as a constitutive feature of their self-differentiation (i.e., as the condition for the generation and spiration of persons), since this would entail a free decision of the persons to receive their identity. God would become Trinity by way of a freely accepted engagement of his being.

Aquinas also underscores the importance of Jesus's perfection of

---

40. White, *The Incarnate Lord,* 277–307.
41. See the arguments of Aquinas, *ST* III, q. 20, aa. 1 and 2.

grace as man. Precisely because his human life is meant to reveal his personal identity as Son, Jesus must have a sufficient human understanding of his own identity and must possess a plenitude of charity in his human heart sufficient to surrender his own life freely to the Father on behalf of the human race.[42] Thomists emphasize then the special character of Jesus's human knowledge as evinced in the Gospels, whereby he is clearly aware of who he is and seems to know of his divine origin as well as the terminus of his temporal mission and its salvific import (Mark 10:45; Matt. 11:27; John 2:25, 3:11, 18:4). Instead of taking these scriptural references as merely post-Paschal theologoumena projected back onto the historical Jesus, one may defend them as ontologically significant indications of Jesus's true identity. This is why authors like Gaine have defended the importance of the traditional teaching that Jesus in his earthly life has the beatific vision, that is to say, the immediate and intuitive understanding of who he is as Lord, by a form of non-inferential knowledge.[43] On this view, Jesus can experience dereliction at the crucifixion and take on effects of our godforsakenness in solidarity with us, but in so doing he still retains a human awareness of his hidden union with the Father and of the eventual triumph of God's design that is unfolding even in the midst of his human suffering (John 19:30; Luke 23:34, 43). His perfection of charity, likewise, is an important facet of his free self-sacrifice in the passion. On Aquinas's view, it is precisely because Jesus gives his life in obedience to God by knowledge and by love that the crucifixion is meritorious as a human act, and can be a source of grace for the whole human race.[44] Christ's human headship in the order of grace (Col. 1:18; Eph. 4:8, 5:23) is grounded in his meritorious self-offering, which in turn presupposes an action of free self-giving.[45] If the Son is subject to lowliness and abasement in the passion, then it is also essential to acknowledge his human un-

---

42. Aquinas, *ST* III, q. 7, a. 1; q. 9, a. 2.

43. See Gaine, *Did the Saviour See the Father? Christ, Salvation, and the Vision of God*, 4–14, 129–78.

44. Aquinas, *ST* III, q. 48, a. 2.

45. Aquinas, *ST* III, q. 7, a. 9; q. 8, aa. 1 and 3.

derstanding of the meaning of the passion and obedient consent to it, even as it unfolds.[46]

Aquinas's Christology presents us with a biblically informed reflection on the mysteries of the life of Christ, influenced by key patristic insights from both Latin and Greek sources. Aquinas is deeply concerned to maintain a Chalcedonian Christology that emphasizes the singular subject of the Son and the distinct two natures in which he personally subsists, while noting many ways that the human nature is subordinate to the divine nature and thereby expressive of the divine person. When this approach is re-appropriated in the modern context, one can see some motifs that converge with those of the modern kenotic Christological tradition. However, a clear difference emerges regarding the distinction of natures in Christ. On Aquinas's view the divine nature remains in many respects transcendent of and dissimilar to the human nature of Christ, even within the hypostatic union. There is a soteriological importance to this point of emphasis. The divine identity of Christ is not altered or sundered by the passion but is dynamically active in the crucifixion, even in the midst of God's human suffering. His human abasement does not provide an analogy for the inner life of God as such, but simply is the human suffering of God. The perfection of Christ's human understanding and love in his passion, meanwhile, are also important, since they indicate in a distinctly human way his deeper divine union with the Father.

CONCLUSION

Paradoxical though it may seem, the historical work of de Lubac and the dogmatic projects of Barth, Rahner, and von Balthasar paved the way for a new appropriation of Aquinas in a contemporary key. By their emphasis on the creative re-appropriation of classical themes in theology within a modern landscape, they made space for new projects of this kind. Ressourcement Thomism func-

---

46. Aquinas, *ST* III, q. 22, a. 3, and White, *The Incarnate Lord*, 353–59, 367–72.

tions as a sociological category for an emerging trend toward the recovery and inventive use of ideas derived from the work of Thomas Aquinas. That such a restatement of Thomistic themes can exist
anew in novel theological circumstances, and with new resonances
or points of inflection, is a sign of the living vitality of Thomism as
an intellectual tradition of enduring character. This tradition itself
is a testament to the depth and perpetual pertinence of Aquinas's
philosophical and theological insight. It is also a sign of the chronic vigor of traditional Christian theological ideas more generally,
which re-emerge in their perennial intellectual value and power of
explanation, through a variety of intellectual idioms and forms of
expression from age to age.

Bibliography

―――――:―――――

WORKS BY THOMAS AQUINAS

De malo. Vol. 23 of *Sancti Thomae de Aquino opera omnia.* Leonine Edition. Rome and Paris: Leonine Commission and J. Vrin, 1982.

De veritate. Vol. 22 of *Sancti Thomae de Aquino opera omnia.* Leonine Edition. Rome: Editori di San Tommaso, 1975–76.

Summa contra Gentiles. Vols. 13–15 of *Sancti Thomae Aquinatis opera omnia.* Leonine Edition. Rome: R. Garroni, 1918–30.

Summa theologiae. Vols. 4–12 of *Sancti Thomae Aquinatis opera omnia.* Leonine Edition. Rome: 1888–1906.

TRANSLATIONS OF WORKS BY THOMAS AQUINAS

Commentary on Aristotle's Metaphysics. Translated by J. P. Rowan. South Bend, IN: Dumb Ox Books, 1995.

Summa contra Gentiles II. Translated by J. Anderson. Garden City, NY: Doubleday, 1956.

Summa Theologica. Translated by the English Dominican Province. New York: Benziger Brothers, 1947.

Theological Compendium. Translated by Cyril Vollert. St. Louis, MO: B. Herder Book, 1947.

CONCILIAR, MAGISTERIAL, AND PAPAL WORKS

Catechism of the Catholic Church. 2nd ed. Vatican City: Libreria Editrice Vaticana, 1997.

Denzinger, Heinrich. *Compendium of Creeds, Definitions, and Declarations on Matters of Faith and Morals,* 43rd ed. Edited by P. Hünermann, edited for English by R. Fastiggi and A. E. Nash. San Francisco: Ignatius Press, 2012.

Benedict XVI. *Deus caritas est.* Encyclical Letter. December 25, 2005.

Francis. *Veritatis gaudium*. Apostolic Constitution. December 27, 2017.

John Paul II. *Fides et ratio*. Encyclical Letter. September 14, 1998.

———. *Novo millennio ineunte*. Apostolic Letter. January 6, 2001.

Leo XIII. *Aeterni Patris*. Encyclical Letter. August 4, 1879.

Paul VI. *Optatam totius*. Decree on Priestly Training. October 28, 1965.

Vatican Council I. *Dei Filius*. Dogmatic Constitution. April 24, 1870.

Vatican Council II. *Dei Verbum*. Dogmatic Constitution. November 18, 1965.

———. *Gaudium et spes*. Pastoral Constitution. December 7, 1965.

———. *Lumen gentium*. Dogmatic Constitution. November 21, 1964.

———. *Unitatis redintegratio*. Decree on Ecumenism. November 21, 1964.

CLASSICAL AND MODERN WORKS

Aertsen, Jan. *Medieval Philosophy and the Transcendentals: The Case of Thomas Aquinas*. Leiden: Brill, 1996.

Anatolios, Khaled. *Retrieving Nicaea: The Development and Meaning of Trinitarian Doctrine*. Grand Rapids, MI: Baker Academic, 2011.

Aristotle. *The Complete Works of Aristotle*. Edited by J. Barnes. Translated by W. D. Ross. 2 vols. Princeton: Princeton University Press, 1984.

Ashley, Benedict. *The Way toward Wisdom: An Interdisciplinary and Intercultural Introduction to Metaphysics*. Notre Dame, IN: University of Notre Dame Press, 2006.

Augustine. *The Trinity*. Edited by J. E. Rotelle. Translated by E. Hill. Hyde Park, NY: New City Press, 1991.

Ayres, Lewis. *Augustine and the Trinity*. Cambridge: Cambridge University Press, 2010.

Balthasar, Hans Urs von. *Epilogue*. Translated by E. Oakes. San Francisco: Ignatius Press, 2004.

———. *Explorations in Theology*, vols. 1–5. Translated by A. V. Littledale, A. Dru, and others. San Francisco: Ignatius Press, 1989–2014.

———. *The Moment of Christian Witness* (*Cordula oder der Ernstfall*). Translated by R. Beckley. San Francisco: Ignatius Press, 1994.

———. *Theo-Drama Theological-Dramatic Theory*. Vol. 3, *The Dramatis Personae: Persons in Christ*. Translated by G. Harrison. San Francisco: Ignatius Press, 1992.

———. *Theo-Drama Theological-Dramatic Theory*. Vol. 4, *The Action*. Translated by G. Harrison. San Francisco: Ignatius Press, 1994.

———. *Theo-Logic: Theological Logical Theory*. Vol. 2, *The Truth of God*. Translated by A. Walker. San Francisco: Ignatius Press, 2004.

———. *The Theology of Karl Barth: Exposition and Interpretation*. Translated by E. Oakes. San Francisco: Ignatius Press, 1992.

Barth, Karl. *Church Dogmatics*. Edited by G. W. Bromiley and T. F. Torrance. 4 vols. Edinburgh: T&T Clark, 1936–75.

———. *Letters 1961–1968*. Translated by G. W. Bromiley. Grand Rapids, MI: Eerdmans, 1981.

Betz, John. "Beyond the Sublime: The Aesthetics of the Analogy of Being." *Modern Theology* 21 (2005): 367–411 and *Modern Theology* 22 (2006): 1–50.

Blankenhorn, Bernhard. *The Mystery of Union with God: Dionysian Mysticism in Albert the Great and Thomas Aquinas*. Washington, DC: The Catholic University of America Press, 2015.

Bonaventure. *Commentaria in quatuor libros Sententiarum*, 4 vols. Quaracchi: Ex Typographia Collegii S. Bonaventurae, 1882–89.

Bonino, Serge-Thomas. *Dieu, "Celui Qui Est"- De Deo ut Uno*. Paris: Parole et Silence, 2016.

Bouyer, Louis. *Mysterion: Du mystère à la mystique*. Paris: Les Éditions du Cerf, 2017.

Bulgakov, Sergius. *The Lamb of God*. Translated by B. Jakim. Grand Rapids, MI: Eerdmans, 2008.

Cessario, Romanus. *Introduction to Moral Theology*, rev. ed. Washington, DC: The Catholic University of America Press, 2013.

———. *The Moral Virtues and Theological Ethics*, 2nd ed. Notre Dame, IN: University of Notre Dame Press, 2008.

Chenu, Marie-Dominique. *Toward Understanding Saint Thomas*. Translated by A.-M. Landry and D. Hughes. Chicago: Henry Regnery, 1964.

Congar, Yves. *My Journal of the Council*. Translated by M. J. Ronayne and M. C. Boulding. Edited by D. Minns. Collegeville, MN: Liturgical Press, 2012.

———. *Situation et Taches Présentes de la Théologie*. Paris: Cerf, 1967.

———. *La tradition et les traditions*, 2 vols. Paris: A. Fayard, 1960–1963.

Cottier, Georges. *Les chemins de la raison: Questions d'épistémologie théologique et philosophique*. Paris: Parole et Silence, 1997.

Cyril of Alexandria. *The Christological Controversy*. Edited and translated by R. A. Norris, Jr. Philadelphia: Fortress Press, 1980.

Daley, Brian. *God Visible: Patristic Christology Reconsidered*. Oxford: Oxford University Press, 2018.

de la Soujeole, Benoit-Dominique. *Introduction to the Mystery of the Church*. Translated by M. J. Miller. Washington, DC: The Catholic University of America Press, 2016.

———. *Le sacrement de la communion: essai d'ecclésiologie fondamentale*. Paris: Cerf, 1998.

Del Prado, Norbert. *De veritate fundamentali philosophiae christianae*. Fribourg: Consociatio Sancti Pauli, 1911.

Dewan, Lawrence. "The Existence of God: Can It Be Demonstrated?" *Nova et Vetera* (English edition) 10, no. 3 (2012): 731–56.

———. *Form and Being: Studies in Thomistic Metaphysics*. Washington, DC: The Catholic University of America Press, 2006.

Echeverria, E. J. "Hierarchy of Truths Revisited." *African Journals Online (AJOL)* (2015): 11–35.

Emery, Gilles. "Essentialism or Personalism in the Treatise on God in St. Thomas Aquinas?" *The Thomist* 64, no. 4 (2000): 521–63.

——. *The Trinitarian Theology of St. Thomas Aquinas.* Translated by F. Murphy. Oxford: Oxford University Press, 2010.

——. *Trinity, Church, and the Human Person.* Naples, FL: Sapientia Press, 2007.

——. *Trinity in Aquinas.* Naples, FL: Sapientia Press, 2006

Fabro, Cornelio. "De Doctrina S. Thomae in Scholis Catholicis Promovenda," *Acta et Documenta* IV/II/1 (Typis Polyglottis Vaticanis, 1961), 177–89.

——. *God in Exile: Modern Atheism. A Study of the Internal Dynamic of Modern Atheism, from Its Roots in the Cartesian Cogito to the Present Day.* Translated by A. Gibson. New York: Newman, 1968; Italian ed. 1964.

——. *La svolta antropologica di Karl Rahner, Opere Complete* 25. Rome: EDIVI Press, 2011.

——. *Participation et causalité selon saint Thomas d'Aquin.* Louvain: Publications Universitaires de Louvain, 1961.

Feingold, Lawrence. *The Natural Desire to See God according to St. Thomas Aquinas and His Interpreters,* 2nd ed. Naples, FL: Sapientia Press, 2010.

Frei, Hans. *Types of Christian Theology.* Edited by G. Hunsinger and W. C. Placher. New Haven: Yale University Press, 1992.

Friedman, Russell. *Intellectual Traditions at the Medieval University: The Use of Philosophical Psychology in Trinitarian Theology among the Franciscans and Dominicans, 1250–1350,* 2 vols. Leiden: Brill, 2012.

——. *Medieval Trinitarian Thought from Aquinas to Ockham.* Cambridge: Cambridge University Press, 2013.

Gaine, Simon F. *Did the Saviour See the Father? Christ, Salvation, and the Vision of God.* London: T&T Clark, 2015.

Gilson, Étienne. *L'Être et l'Essence,* 2nd ed. Paris: J. Vrin, 1972.

Gregory of Nazianzus. *On God and Christ. The Five Theological Orations and Two Letters to Cledonius.* Translated by Frederick Williams and Lionel Wickham. Yonkers, NY: St. Vladimir's Seminary Press, 2002.

Hegel, G. W. F. *Lectures on the Philosophy of Religion, One-Volume Edition: The Lectures of 1827.* Translated by R. F. Brown, P. C. Hodgson, J. M. Stewart. Oxford: Clarendon Press, 2006.

Heidegger, Martin. *The Fundamental Concepts of Metaphysics: World, Finitude, Solitude.* Translated W. McNeill and N. Walker. Bloomington: Indiana University Press, 2001.

Hütter, Reinhard. *Bound for Beatitude: A Thomistic Study in Eschatology and Ethics.* Washington, DC: The Catholic University of America Press, 2019.

——. *Dust Bound for Heaven: Explorations in the Theology of Thomas Aquinas* Grand Rapids, MI: Eerdmans, 2012.

John Damascene. *The Orthodox Faith.* In *Nicene and Post-Nicene Fathers, Second Series,* vol. 9. Edited by P. Schaff and H. Wace, translated by E. W. Watson and L. Pullan. Buffalo, NY: Christian Literature Publishing, 1899.

Johnson, Keith. *Karl Barth and the Analogia Entis.* London: T&T Clark, 2011.

Journet, Charles. *Les Septs Paroles du Christ au Croix*. Paris: Éditions du Seuil, 1954.

Kant, Immanuel. *The Critique of Pure Reason*. Translated by N. K. Smith. London: Macmillan, 1990.

———. *Religion within the Boundaries of Mere Reason*. Translated by A. Wood and G. di Giovanni. Cambridge: Cambridge University Press, 1998.

Kasper, Walter. *The Absolute in History: The Philosophy and Theology of History in Schelling's Late Philosophy*. Translated by K. Wolff. New York: Paulist Press, 2018.

———. *The God of Jesus Christ*. Translated by M. J. O'Connell. New York: Crossroad, 1989.

Keating, James F., and Thomas Joseph White, eds. *Divine Impassibility and the Mystery of Human Suffering*. Grand Rapids, MI: Eerdmans, 2009.

Ker, Ian. *Newman on Vatican II*. Oxford: Oxford University Press, 2014.

Komonchak, Joseph A. "Thomism and the Second Vatican Council." In *Continuity and Plurality in Catholic Theology: Essays in Honor of Gerald A. McCool, S.J.*, edited by A. J. Cemera, 53–73. Fairfield, CT: Sacred Heart University Press, 1998.

Legge, Dominic. *The Trinitarian Christology of St. Thomas Aquinas*. Oxford: Oxford University Press, 2016.

Le Guillou, M. J. *Christ and Church: A Theology of the Mystery*. Translated by C. Schaldenbrand. New York: Desclee, 1966.

Leinsle, Ulrich G. *Introduction to Scholastic Theology*. Translated by M. Miller. Washington, DC: The Catholic University of America Press, 2010.

Levering, Matthew. *Engaging the Doctrine of Creation: Cosmos, Creatures, and the Wise and Good Creator*. Grand Rapids, MI: Baker Academic, 2017.

———. *Engaging the Doctrine of Revelation*. Grand Rapids, MI: Baker Academic, 2014.

———. *Participatory Biblical Exegesis: A Theology of Biblical Interpretation*. Notre Dame, IN: University of Notre Dame Press, 2008.

———. *Scripture and Metaphysics: Aquinas and the Renewal of Trinitarian Theology*. Oxford: Wiley-Blackwell, 1994.

Loisy, Alfred. *Prelude to the Modernist Crisis: The "Firmin" Articles of Alfred Loisy*. Translated by Christine Thirlway. Edited by C. J. T. Talar. Oxford: Oxford University Press, 2010.

Lonergan, Bernard. *Collected Works of Bernard Lonergan*. Edited by F. Crowe, R. Doran, and others. Toronto: University of Toronto Press, 2000–present.

Lynch, Reginald. *The Cleansing of the Heart: The Sacraments as Instrumental Causes in the Thomistic Tradition*. Washington, DC: The Catholic University of America Press, 2017.

MacIntyre, Alasdair. *After Virtue: A Study in Moral Theory*, 3rd ed. Notre Dame, IN: University of Notre Dame Press, 1997.

———. *First Principles, Final Ends, and Contemporary Philosophical Issues*. Milwaukee: Marquette University Press, 1990.

——. *Three Rival Versions of Moral Inquiry*. Notre Dame, IN: University of Notre Dame Press, 1990.

Marion, Jean-Luc. "Saint Thomas d'Aquin et l'onto-théo-logie." *Revue Thomiste* 95 (1995): 31–66.

Maritain, Jacques. *Distinguer pour Unir ou Les Degrés du Savoir*. Paris: Désclée de Brouwer, 1932. *The Degrees of Knowledge*. Translated by G. B. Phelan. Notre Dame, IN: University of Notre Dame Press, 1995.

——. *Oeuvres Complète*, vol. XIII. Fribourg and Paris: Éditions Universitaires and Éditions Saint-Paul, 1992.

Marshall, Bruce D. "The Absolute and the Trinity." *Pro Ecclesia* 13, no. 2 (2014): 147–64.

——. *Christology in Conflict: The Identity of a Savior in Rahner and Barth*. Oxford: Blackwell, 1987.

——. "Personal Distinction in God and the Possibility of Kenosis." *Angelicum* 98, no. 1 (2021): 65–104.

——. "The Unity of the Triune God: Reviving an Ancient Question." *The Thomist* 74 (2010): 1–32.

McCormack, Bruce L., and Thomas Joseph White, eds. *Aquinas and Barth: An Unofficial Catholic Protestant Ecumenical Dialogue*. Grand Rapids, MI: Eerdmans, 2013.

Meyendorff, John. *A Study of Gregory Palamas*. Translated G. Lawrence. Crestwood, NY: St. Vladimir's Seminary Press, 1974.

Moltmann, Jürgen. *The Crucified God: The Cross of Christ as the Foundation and Criticism of Christian Life*. Translated by R. A. Wilson and J. Bowden. San Francisco: Harper and Row, 1974.

Nagel, Thomas. *Mind and Cosmos: Why the Materialist Neo-Darwinian Conception of Nature Is Almost Certainly False*. New York: Oxford University Press, 2012.

Newman, John Henry. *An Essay on Development of Christian Doctrine*. Notre Dame, IN: University of Notre Dame Press, 1989.

Nichols, Aidan. *From Newman to Congar: The Idea of Development from the Victorians to the Second Vatican Council*. Edinburgh: T&T Clark, 1990.

Nicolas, Jean-Hervé. *Catholic Dogmatic Theology, A Synthesis. Book I, On the Trinitarian Mystery of God*. Translated by M. K. Minerd. Washington, DC: The Catholic University of America Press, 2022.

Oderberg, David S. *Real Essentialism*. New York: Routledge, 2007.

Pannenberg, Wolfhart. *Theology and the Philosophy of Science*. Translated by F. McDonagh. Philadelphia: Westminster John Knox Press, 1976.

Pekarske, Daniel. *Abstracts of Karl Rahner's Theological Investigations 1–23*. Milwaukee: Marquette University Press, 2003.

Perrier, Emmanuel. *L'attrait divin: La doctrine de l'opération et le gouvernement des créatures chez saint Thomas d'Aquin*. Paris: Parole et Silence, 2019.

——. *La fécondité en Dieu: La puissance notionnelle dans la Trinité selon saint Thomas d'Aquin*. Paris: Parole et Silence, 2009.

Phelan, Owen M. "Horizontal and Vertical Theologies: 'Sacraments' in the Works of Paschasius Radbertus and Ratramnus of Corbie." *The Harvard Theological Review* 103, no. 3 (July 2010): 271–89.

Pinckaers, Servais. *The Sources of Christian Ethics*, 3rd ed. Translated by M. T. Noble Washington, DC: The Catholic University of America Press, 1995.

Przywara, Erich. *Analogia Entis: Metaphysics: Original Structure and Universal Rhythm*. Translated by J. Betz and D. B. Hart. Grand Rapids, MI: Eerdmans, 2014.

Rahner, Karl. *The Church and the Sacraments*. Translated by W. J. O'Hara. New York: Herder and Herder, 1963.

———. *Foundations of Christian Faith: An Introduction to the Idea of Christianity*. Translated by W. Dych. New York: Crossroad, 1978.

———. *The Trinity*. Translated by J. Donceel. London: Continuum, 2001.

Ratzinger, Joseph. *Eschatology: Death and Eternal Life*. Translated by M. Waldstein and A. Nichols. Washington, DC: The Catholic University of America Press, 1988.

———. *"In the Beginning ...": A Catholic Understanding of the Story of Creation and the Fall*. Translated by B. Ramsey. Grand Rapids, MI: Eerdmans, 1998.

———. *Introduction to Christianity*. Translated by J. R. Foster. San Francisco: Ignatius Press, 2000.

———. *Principles of Catholic Theology: Building Stones for a Fundamental Theology*. Translated by Mary Frances McCarthy. San Francisco: Ignatius Press, 1987.

Reno, R. R. "Rahner the Restorationist: Karl Rahner's Time Has Passed." *First Things*. May 2013.

Schenk, Richard. *Revelations of Humanity Anthropological Dimensions of Theological Controversies*. Washington, DC: The Catholic University of America Press, 2022.

———. *Soundings in the History of a Hope: New Studies on Thomas Aquinas*. Naples, FL: Sapientia Press, 2016.

Schleiermacher, Friedrich. *The Christian Faith*, 2 vols. Edited by H. R. Mackintosh and J. S. Stewart. New York: Harper and Row, 1963.

Schillebeeckx, Edward. *Revelation and Theology*, vols. I and II. New York: Sheed and Ward, 1967.

Söhngen, Gottlieb. "The Analogy of Faith: Likeness to God from Faith Alone?" Translated by K. Oakes. *Pro Ecclesia* 21 (2012): 56–76.

———. "The Analogy of Faith: Unity in the Science of Faith." Translated by K. Oakes, *Pro Ecclesia* 21 (2012): 169–94.

te Velde, Rudi. *Aquinas on God: The 'Divine Science' of the "Summa Theologiae"*. Aldershot: Ashgate, 2006.

Van Steenberghen, Fernand. *La Philosophie au XIIIe Siècle*. Louvain: Éditions Peeters, 1991.

Vijgen, Jörgen. *The Status of Eucharistic Accidents "sine subiecto": An Historical Survey up to Thomas Aquinas and Selected Reactions*. Berlin: Walter de Gruyter, 2013.

von Balthasar, Hans Urs. *See* Balthasar, Hans Urs von

Wallace, William A. *The Modeling of Nature: Philosophy of Science and Philosophy of Nature in Synthesis*. Washington, DC: The Catholic University of America Press, 1996.

Weigel, George. "Rescuing *Gaudium et Spes*: The New Humanism of John Paul II." *Nova et Vetera* (English edition) 8 (2010): 251–67.

White, Thomas Joseph. "The *analogia fidei* in Catholic Theology." *International Journal of Systematic Theology* 22, no. 4 (2020): 512–37.

———, ed. *The Analogy of Being: Invention of the Anti-Christ or Wisdom of God?* Grand Rapids, MI: Eerdmans, 2011.

———. "Dyotheletism and the Instrumental Human Consciousness of Jesus." *Pro Ecclesia* 17, no. 4 (2008): 396–422.

———. *The Incarnate Lord: A Thomistic Study in Christology*. Washington, DC: The Catholic University of America Press, 2015.

———. "*Ressourcement* Thomism." In *The New Cambridge Companion to Christian Doctrine*, edited by Michael Allen, 352–70. Cambridge: Cambridge University Press, 2022.

———. *The Trinity: On the Nature and Mystery of the One God*. Washington, DC: The Catholic University of America Press, 2022.

———. *Wisdom in the Face of Modernity: A Study in Thomistic Natural Theology*, 2nd ed. Naples, FL: Sapientia Press, 2016.

Wippel, John F. *Metaphysical Themes in Thomas Aquinas II*. Washington, DC: The Catholic University of America Press, 2007.

Person Index

——— : ———

Aertsen, Jan: 82n40, 129n11, 166
Alexander of Hales: 94
Anatolios, Khaled: 62n2, 96n4, 166
Apollinarius: 18–19, 117
Aristotle: 6–7, 17–18, 81n35, 82n39, 96,
    128, 166
Ashley, Benedict: 136n21, 166
Athanasius: 99
Augustine: 12, 70–72, 99, 120, 150,
    153n18, 156, 157n29, 166

Baius, Michael: 65n6,
Báñez, Domingo: 145
Barth, Karl: 28n13, 30–34, 38–42, 57, 92,
    97n8, 98–101, 102n16, 102n17, 103–9,
    111–15, 117–18, 120, 142, 148, 153–55,
    159, 163, 166
Benedict XVI: 109n29, 144, 166. See also
    Ratzinger, Joseph
Betz, John: 37n35, 102, 167
Billuart, Charles René: 124
Blankenhorn, Bernhard: 149–50, 167
Boethius: 120
Bonaventure: 71–72, 111, 140, 167
Bonino, Serge-Thomas: 147–49, 167
Bouyer, Louis: 51n57, 60n1, 167
Bulgakov, Sergius: 113, 114n38, 115, 148,
    167

Cajetan, Thomas del Vio: 145
Calvin, John: 106, 112n34
Catherine of Siena: 111
Cessario, Romanus: 146, 167
Chenu, Marie-Dominique: 14, 15n15,
    83n41, 132, 138, 143, 145, 167
Congar, Yves: 49n56, 94n1, 122, 124–26,
    132, 167
Cottier, Georges: 53n59, 167
Cyril of Alexandria: 73, 112n34, 167

Daley, Brian: 63n3, 96n4, 167
Daniélou, Jean: 143–44
de la Soujeole, Benoit-Dominique:
    151, 167
de Lubac, Henri: 51n57, 91, 132, 143–44,
    150–51, 163
del Prado, Norbert: 130, 131n16, 167
Dewan, Lawrence: 7n3, 100n11, 167

Echeverria, E. J.: 88n45, 168
Emery, Gilles: 72n16, 147–49, 156, 168

Fabro, Cornelio: 28n13, 123–26, 157n10,
    168
Feingold, Lawrence: 149–51, 168
Foucault, Michel: 134,
Francis of Assisi: 111
Franzelin, Johann Baptist: 143
Frei, Hans: 25n1, 168

173

Subject Index

agent intellect: 8, 18, 127
analogia entis: 33n9, 37–42, 49, 52, 5
   6–58, 101–5, 108–10, 115, 119, 123,
   160
analogia fidei: 25–58, 108
apophaticism (negative theology):
   61, 69–70

beatific vision: 5, 116, 149, 162

Christocentrism: 16, 41
Christology: 23, 28–29, 40, 94, 96n4,
   99, 110, 112, 121, 149, 158n32, 159;
   Chalcedonian, 25, 63, 73, 97, 107, 109,
   118–19, 143, 163; dyothelitist, 73, 115,
   120, 143
Council of Chalcedon: 93, 160n38
Council of Nicaea: 96, 109
creation: 5, 8, 13, 15–17, 20, 24, 31–33, 35,
   38, 44–46, 51, 54, 60, 64n5, 75–76, 83,
   88–90, 95, 97n8, 102 3, 105–9, 115n40,
   124, 128, 136, 138–9, 144, 154, 156
creed: 13, 14n11, 16n16, 19, 23–24, 50–51,
   65n6, 67, 97, 103, 110

Dei Verbum: 10n9, 44n49, 66, 93
development of doctrine: 48, 66, 79,
   81, 94n1
dialectic: 17–20, 22, 35, 39, 105, 114, 127,
   132, 147

divine economy: 15, 46, 51, 60, 138
divine essence/divine nature: 27n9,
   32n26, 35, 63, 71–72, 78, 112, 113n35,
   114n38, 115, 118–20, 131, 154, 159–61,
   163
divine mission: 148

Enlightenment: 25, 49, 143–44
eschatology: 2, 15, 46, 49, 51, 54, 60, 84,
   87, 127, 149–51
Eucharist: 30n18, 35, 51, 60, 63–64, 67–
   68, 74–75, 84–89
exitus-reditus: 14, 16, 46, 83n41, 138

fideism: 123–24
first principles: 6–9
First Vatican Council: 41n43, 58, 98n8,
   101n13
form and matter (hylomorphism): 6–8,
   35, 57, 124, 128, 150
Fourth Lateran Council: 75

God-consciousness: 27
grace: 1, 3, 5, 8–10, 14–16, 19–20, 23–24,
   26, 28–29, 34–37, 39, 42–44, 46, 50–55,
   57–60, 64–65, 67–68, 76–80, 83–84,
   86–89, 93, 97–98, 100–4, 110, 114, 116,
   134, 141, 144, 146, 150–52, 154, 156, 162
idioms, communication of: 112, 113n35,
   115, 120, 149

incarnation: 1, 13–17, 19, 24, 32–33, 38–39, 41, 43, 45–46, 51, 60, 63, 84–86, 88–89, 96, 102–3, 113–14, 139, 154, 157–58

Israel: 2, 9, 13, 22–24, 41, 43, 45–46, 51, 60, 88

kataphaticism (positive theology): 61, 67–70

kenosis: 33, 110, 112–14, 115n40, 118n44, 119, 142, 159–63

Lumen gentium: 17, 23

Mariology: 5, 20, 23, 103

metaphysics: 6n2, 6–8, 25, 31–32, 34–35, 37–39, 41, 54–55, 57, 68, 92, 95–99, 100, 102–5, 109, 119, 124, 128–31, 133, 136, 139, 144, 147, 150

mystery/mysteries: 1–2, 4, 8, 11–16, 19, 23–24, 26–29, 32–33, 39, 41–43, 45–46, 50–92, 95–97, 102, 104n23, 108, 110, 115, 117, 119n45, 120, 130–31, 138–39, 142–44, 147–48, 150–51, 154, 157–59, 163

ontology: 6n2, 6n3, 7, 16, 18–19, 29n17, 30–35, 38–40, 42–47, 51–52, 57–58, 64n5, 65, 68, 74–75, 78, 80–81, 83, 85, 88–89, 94, 97–100, 102–4, 106–7, 110, 112–15, 155, 157–58, 161–62

passion of Jesus Christ: 13, 16n16, 111n31, 162–63

philosophy: 3, 18–19, 23, 31–32, 34–37, 40, 53, 55, 57, 69, 91–93, 99–100, 104–13, 127, 129–31, 133–35, 136n22, 144

praeambula fidei: 54, 100

resurrection of Jesus Christ: 2, 13, 15,

16n16, 17, 30, 41, 43–44, 60, 84, 86, 114n38, 130, 157–59

revelation: 1–5, 8–11, 13, 19, 24, 27, 31, 34–36, 38–44, 47–49, 51–57, 60–61, 66, 80, 84–85, 88–89, 91, 93–96, 98n8, 99, 101, 103–10, 117, 123, 128–30, 138, 142, 144, 153–54, 159

sacra doctrina: 3, 8, 9, 12, 14, 31, 35, 41, 57, 91–121, 129, 147

sacraments: 2, 13–15, 29–30, 35, 43, 51, 60, 64, 80, 84, 87–89, 102–4, 139, 141, 150–52

schools of theology: 4, 9, 11, 68, 70, 94, 110

Second Vatican Council: 5, 10n9, 17, 20–21, 23, 44n49, 48, 66, 84n43, 88n45, 93, 122, 126, 131–32, 144, 151

soul: 2–4, 8, 18–19, 35, 45, 54, 56, 65, 73–79, 84, 86–87, 105n24, 111n31, 127–28, 130, 138

supernatural-existential: 28, 151, 152

Thomism (or Thomistic tradition): 4, 9, 12, 18, 22–25, 39, 57, 70, 78, 87, 91–95, 97–98, 104, 109, 111, 120–64

tradition: 2, 4, 6, 8–12, 19–26, 31, 34–37, 42, 44, 47, 49–51, 56–57, 67, 80, 88n45, 89–90, 92, 99–100, 103, 105–7, 109–12, 114–15, 118–21, 123, 128–30, 132–33, 137–38, 141, 145, 149, 151–52, 154, 160, 162–64

Trinity: 1–2, 4–6, 13–17, 20, 24, 26, 27n9, 28, 33, 35, 38, 41, 43, 44, 46, 51, 53–54, 58, 62, 67, 70, 71, 78, 80, 83–89, 95–96, 102–4, 110, 112–14, 119–20, 127, 130–31, 140, 142–43, 148–49, 153–61

Virgin Mary: 2, 16n16, 23–24, 51, 60, 84, 102, 104, 105n24

Series Editors: Matthew Levering
Thomas Joseph White, OP

Reading the Song of Songs with St. Thomas Aquinas
Serge-Thomas Bonino, OP
Translated by Andrew Levering with Matthew Levering

Divine Speech in Human Words
Thomistic Engagements with Scripture
Emmanuel Durand, OP
Edited by Matthew K. Minerd

Revelations of Humanity
Anthropological Dimensions of Theological Controversies
Richard Schenk, OP

The Trinity
On the Nature and Mystery of the One God
Thomas Joseph White, OP

Catholic Dogmatic Theology, A Synthesis
Book I, On the Trinitarian Mystery of God
Jean-Hervé Nicolas, OP
Translated by Matthew K. Minerd

A Thomistic Christocentrism
Recovering the Carmelites of Salamanca on the Logic of the Incarnation
Dylan Schrader